ADVANCE PRAISE

"I have been waiting for this book for my whole life! You have in your hands the number one leadership tool for success: the power and method of building connections and trust. Liesbeth's world-class skills have been honed with her boots on the ground. She is an extraordinary coach, able to uncover the real issues and provide you with practical tools to address them like few others. Connect, Inspire, Grow is a vital resource for leaders in all industries, a requirement for building skills and enabling tremendous outcomes."

—**LINDA SCOTT**, Namibian High Commissioner to the United Kingdom and Northern Ireland; Namibian High Commissioner to Malta; Namibian Ambassador to Greece and Ireland and The Sovereign Military Order of Malta

"Liesbeth van der Linden guides you through the essential ingredients for successful global leadership. Her guidance in building the foundations to connect and shape a high-performing team in today's dispersed working environments is a must-read for all aspiring leaders of today and tomorrow."

—**MICHAEL DREW**, eCommerce Head, ASEAN and South Pacific at The Coca-Cola Company

"A powerful framework for leaders in a global role to connect, inspire, and grow their teams for long-term success. Experience what changes when you start leading from the inside out and start connecting with people at a deeper level."

—ELBERTI UITERWAAL-POSTMA,
Senior Vice President Global Quality & Support at First Advantage

CONNECT

INSPIRE

GROW

CONNECT

INSPIRE

GROW

The Executive's Framework
for the First 100 Days

LIESBETH van der LINDEN

The names and identifying details of certain individuals have been changed to protect their privacy.

LIONCREST
PUBLISHING

CONTENTS

To Papa

INTRODUCTION

"I'm not telling you it's going to be easy. I'm telling you it's going to be worth it."

—ART WILLIAMS

IF YOU'RE HOLDING THIS BOOK, YOU'VE LIKELY BEEN OFFERED an exciting opportunity to further your career in an immersive global leadership role. You're here because leadership is a responsibility you value highly, and you're looking to start the next chapter of your life on the right foot. If this is the case, I'd like to begin by congratulating you on how far you've already come. Like many people, you may attribute the success you've achieved thus far to specific accomplishments. In reality, the quality of your thinking has brought you to where you are today, at the precipice of a bold chance to help shape the future of your organization and change the lives of everyone you touch. To arrive here is no small feat.

This book was written primarily for executives gearing up to embark on a new global role. My goal is to help set you up for success so you can make the most of every step of the experience. By following the 100-day Connect, Inspire, Grow framework I teach in my work, you'll learn what's required to lead your new team effectively, how to avoid the pitfalls encountered by those who came before you, and where to focus your attention throughout the process. With the average cost of an expat assignment totaling around $311,000 per year, it's in the best interest of you and your company that you enter your new role well prepared.

Research from the INSEAD business school estimates that 40 percent of all overseas deployments fail. That's a staggering number no executive entering an international position can afford to ignore. The most common reasons for failure include an inability to adapt to the new culture, a lack of support from one's organization in the host country, and personal challenges related to living abroad. If you've already stepped into a global leadership position and are finding yourself in the thick of such problems, this book can be beneficial for you as well. You may have lost your initial enthusiasm after not making the progress you anticipated, not getting the results you hoped for, or not having the impact you would've liked so far. You may feel stuck, lost in the fog of the process, and desperate to change the trajectory your team is currently on. There may be unexpected aspects of your new role that differ greatly from what your previous role entailed. This can all be discouraging and frustrating, but none of it has to be a death knell. The power to change your situation is in your hands and available to you today. This book will provide you with direct guidance on how to harness it.

Being an effective leader in today's global environment is certainly challenging, especially for those who are stationed abroad or leading distributed teams. If mastering this process hasn't come naturally to you thus far, you're far from alone. Over the years, I've seen many qualified people who, despite enjoying immense professional success prior to moving overseas, found themselves struggling soon after arrival. One of them, Alex, had been a senior sales executive for a top global consumer products brand. He moved to Shanghai with his wife and three children, energized and bursting with a sense of adventure. He arrived well prepared, having already found a home to rent and good schools for his kids to attend in China. He'd taken a number of cultural training courses and read books on local business etiquette. For all intents and purposes, he was poised to thrive in his new role.

Six months down the road, Alex felt himself hitting a wall and began to wonder whether he'd made a mistake. The members of his team seemed to agree with him on business goals and strategies but weren't delivering the results they needed. Customers were making buying decisions at a glacially slow pace. Worst of all, Alex didn't feel properly supported by the local Chinese staff at his organization. Explaining all the nuanced details of this situation to his bosses at the company's headquarters in the US seemed impossible. Isolated and defeated, Alex lost interest in his work, void of the enthusiasm he'd initially brought to the table. He started complaining frequently, making sweeping generalizations about Chinese people to deflect attention from his doubt and insecurity over his ability to succeed. Eventually, Alex made the decision to move back to his home country with his family, long before completing his contract.

The uncomfortable truth of the matter is that international transitions are bound to get messy regardless of how well you've prepared. Rather than getting derailed by the challenges that arise throughout your assignment, it's better to expect the unexpected prior to departure. With new leadership tools, a framework for action, and a variety of best practices under your belt, you'll be able to shift out of negative mindsets and avoid getting stuck in the weeds of frustration. This book can serve as a valuable resource in such moments, one you can turn to when you feel the need to troubleshoot and steer yourself back in the right direction. Your ability to pivot toward effective solutions in times of difficulty will inspire trust among your team, your organization, and its stakeholders, demonstrating your worth as a valuable asset to their mission.

Many organizations make the mistake of selecting executives to lead teams overseas based solely on their technical competence, but this alone isn't enough to deliver results. Developing skills like self-awareness, open-mindedness, emotional intelligence, and the ability to build trust while connecting with others is equally crucial, if not more so. This is not a book about business strategies or the technical skills necessary for effective leadership. Instead, you'll find in these pages a book about the mind. *Your* mind. In my work, I talk with leaders and observe how they use their minds to achieve amazing results. I also notice how their minds can work against them and stand in the way of progress, to the detriment of themselves and those who follow them.

As I mentioned, the quality of your thinking is what brought you to this point. Everything we say and do starts with our thinking, making our minds the most powerful tool at our disposal. This book is based on the real-world learnings of people who have been deep in the trenches, and who learned the "hard" way. I had to learn the hard way too. Why? Because these kinds of lessons aren't taught to us in business school. At least, they weren't when I got my MBA. Our education systems and business schools spend little to no time on curriculum related to our mindset, behavior, or skills related to communication, emotional intelligence, and

trust. However, these elements are the very glue that holds organizations together. Learning to master them will make or break
your experience. I've seen far too many talented leaders who, like
Alex, were forced to abandon their roles stressed, exhausted, and
demoralized. The good news is that this unfortunate outcome is
completely avoidable and unnecessary.

In Part 1 of this book, I share mental-performance practices you
can use to lay a foundation for success in your new role before
your assignment has even begun. We'll cover introspective work
related to your strengths, values, and mindset. In Part 2, I introduce my three-step framework for the first 100 days, which is
designed to help you *Connect* with your new team members,
Inspire them to succeed, and *Grow* their individual and collective capabilities. The average expat contract lasts a short period
of two to three years. These assignments entail an inherent sense
of urgency to produce results quickly. Chapters three, four, and
five will provide you with the strategies needed to hit the ground
running. Finally, in Part 3, I discuss the seven major challenges
leaders encounter while leading global teams. You'll learn to
navigate tricky situations involving generation gaps, culture
clashes, frustration related to past leadership failures, and other
common sources of conflict.

Having spent fifteen years working abroad, I've not only seen
others make the mistakes described in this book, but have
also made several of them myself. One especially pivotal point
occurred early on in my career in 1998 while I was giving a
presentation in a conference room in Germany. I was twen-
ty-eight years old, had held a management position for four
years with an American company based in Europe, and was no
stranger to leadership in my work. My task was to lead the inte-
gration of the German market's sales support function into my

existing team. Though I had already lived in Germany for over two years, this was the first time I was confronted with challenges related to working in a foreign culture. That day, as I presented the flowcharts I'd prepared and laid out my plan for the new internal sales organization, I felt a cold, hostile energy permeate the room. People exchanged skeptical glances. Eyes rolled. I knew then that my attempts to prepare hadn't resulted in the buy-in I would need.

When I finished that presentation, the German sales team tore it to pieces. They vocally expressed their lack of confidence in my abilities, specifying that I seemed to have no clue how the local market actually worked. I was shocked by their emotional response, only to realize later that these men were still processing the pain of the changes taking place in our organization. When my team took over internal sales support in Germany, their local colleagues in sales, some of whom they had worked with for over twenty years, were made redundant. None of them knew me or my colleagues well, and we, in turn, did not know their customers. Though I was resentful and angry about their harsh way of giving feedback, I knew on a deeper level that they had a point. I was confronted with the reality of everything I'd overlooked in my efforts. The conflict in front of me was about human emotions. Issues of trust and mistrust. In my quest to succeed, I had completely neglected that angle of the situation. I had been managing teams for years but was not yet a leader.

From that moment, I began to shift my approach by asking different questions. How could I effectively influence people? How could I get their buy-in and convince them to follow my lead rather than telling them what they should think or do? With an eye on refining my skills, I enrolled in a leadership development program offered by my company and graduated with distinction, but that wasn't enough to satisfy my desire to improve.

In 2002, I quit my job, studied full time for a year, completed my MBA, and continued my career in management consulting over the following seven years. In 2011, my family and I accepted an opportunity that required us to move to China, where I set up a consulting company to advise investors and local governments on their tourism and leisure projects, which was my first chance to build a business abroad from the ground up. After six years in China, our family moved to Germany. There, I conducted corporate training programs in management and leadership while earning my coaching certification. In 2017, I founded GLTD Ltd., my global executive coaching company. Since then I've dedicated my career to serving global leaders working internationally in the Middle East, Asia, Europe, and Australia.

Over the years, I've noticed how tempting it is for us as global leaders to reduce the challenges of working abroad to culture clashes. We blame local circumstances when problems arise rather than stopping to recalibrate our own approach. We can't force the people we lead to change how they think or feel. We can only change *ourselves* in ways that set them up for success.

It's become more important than ever to look beneath the surface and connect with those we work with at the human level, beyond considerations like culture, age, or technical knowledge. The fallout of the COVID-19 pandemic revealed a great deal about how people's attitudes toward work have evolved in recent years. After the Great Resignation came the War for Talent, resulting in a new normal where professionals prioritized work-life balance and alignment with their personal values. It used to be enough for employers to offer a fair salary, a good benefits package, and a comfortable working environment, but that's no longer the case.

Fundamentally, we all share the same basic desires at work. We want to be seen. We want to be respected. We want to grow. As a global leader entering a new role, you now have the opportunity to communicate with your team in ways that ensure these fundamental needs are met. By connecting with those you lead and building the trust necessary to create those conditions, you'll be far more likely to achieve the results you seek no matter where you're located.

As a leader, it all starts and ends with you. With this in mind, let's begin by exploring the one thing that will gear you and your team members toward success.

PART 1

LEADING OTHERS STARTS WITH LEADING YOURSELF

1

TRAIN YOUR MIND FOR SUCCESS

Your Most Powerful Leadership Tool

"Mind training matters. It is not just a luxury, or a supplementary vitamin for the soul. It determines the quality of every instant of our lives."

—NORMAN DOIDGE

NOW THAT YOU'VE ACCEPTED YOUR ROLE, YOU'RE LIKELY DOING everything you can to set yourself up for a smooth transition. How can you begin creating a foundation for effective teamwork before you've even met your new team? Moving abroad entails all sorts of considerations, from housing to visas to schooling. Apart from ticking these off your checklist, what else can you do to prepare for the challenge ahead of you?

When we accept a new assignment, it's tempting to begin by focusing on the goal of the mission itself. You may be tasked with building an organization from scratch, growing a new market abroad, or fixing a particular problem that's currently hurting your company. You'll likely want to start strategizing on how to kick off the process of change with your team. Before you do, however, let's first take a step back to focus on you, as you'll be the main initiator and driver of that change.

The essence of a great leader is never superficial; it emanates from the inside out. Who are *you*? What is it about you that has put you in this exceptional position? What ingredients can you infuse into your team to drive the process of change and make this mission a success?

In 2010, Green Peak Partners and Cornell's School of Industrial and Labor Relations conducted a study on a range of interpersonal traits among executives. They found that a high self-awareness score was the strongest predictor of overall success. How can we define self-awareness? Put simply, it's a skill that centers on the ability to recognize your thought patterns, triggers, motivators, and different emotional states at any given moment. This involves taking a deep, honest look at yourself, how you respond in certain situations, and why you behave the way that you do.

If self-awareness is the key to leadership success, it makes sense to start preparing for your assignment by exploring how you can become more self-aware.

LEADERSHIP FROM THE INSIDE OUT

Every day, I talk with leaders who use their minds to achieve incredible results. I also see leaders who use their minds in ways that work against them. Let's first look at how your mind and leadership effectiveness are related.

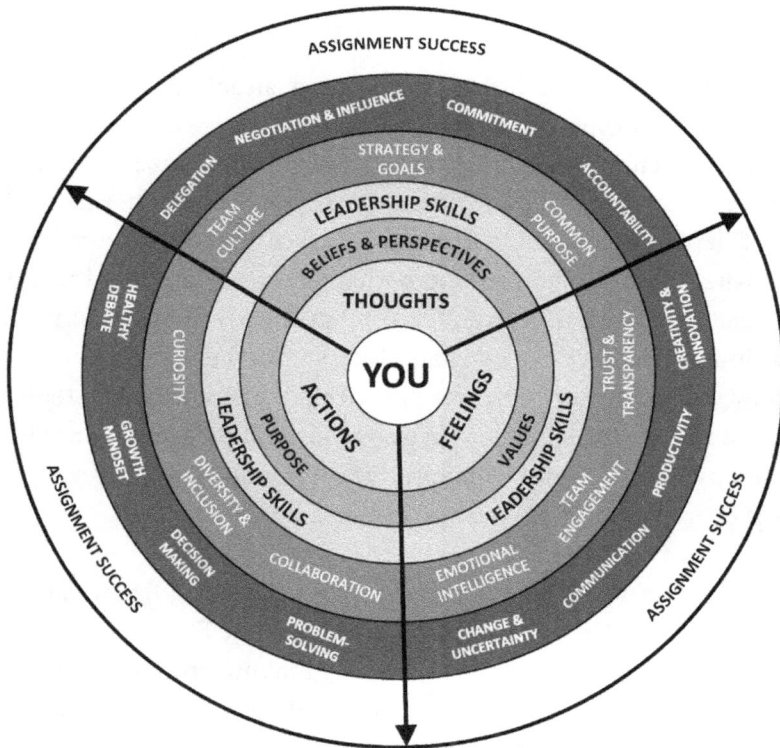

Figure 1. The Core Leadership Methodology

Who are you as a leader? The core of the *Core Leadership Methodology* answer to this question lies in your patterns of thought, feeling, and action. These can either set you up for success or hold you back. If you believe you're powerful, creative, and capable, for example, you're more likely to feel confident and calm. As a result, you'll be better equipped to take on challenges in order to grow. If you see yourself as average, vulnerable, or limited in terms of your potential, however, you might feel worried or fearful. As a result, you'll be more likely to stay in your comfort zone and resist change.

Your thoughts and judgments around situations form your belief system, perspectives, values, and purpose (the second ring), which, in turn, shapes the way you show up as a leader. Your leadership skills (the third ring), which we further discuss in Chapter 2, determine how you interact with your team. This is where you influence the emotional connection, buy-in, and engagement you need from your team. How you lead will have a ripple effect on the next ring, which shows the many aspects of how you and your team interact with people outside the team, including any stakeholders in or outside your organization. The effectiveness of these collaborative interactions will determine the overall success of your assignment.

Over the course of these first two chapters, we're going to take a journey from the center (YOU) outwards. We'll cover how you can optimize your leadership skills by making productive shifts in your thoughts, feelings, and actions. We'll also gain clarity on your purpose, your beliefs, perspectives, and your values. We'll then move outward to the next ring to discuss the leadership skills you'll need to interact with others in ways that ensure your assignment is a success.

YOUR MIND AS A GEARBOX

Let's start at the second ring of the Core Leadership Methodology illustration to explore how your thoughts, feelings, and actions determine the beliefs and perspectives driving your leadership style.

The gearbox is a tool I use with my clients that will allow you to assess your state of mind and quality of thinking. Your decisions, communication style, and the invisible barriers you create for yourself all stem from this place.

The gearbox is inside you. It's inside everyone. Visualizing it can help boost the level of your thinking regardless of your current state of mind. By pinpointing which gear you're currently in, you'll be able to shift to a superior state of mind, allowing you to make better decisions and move past whatever challenges you're facing.

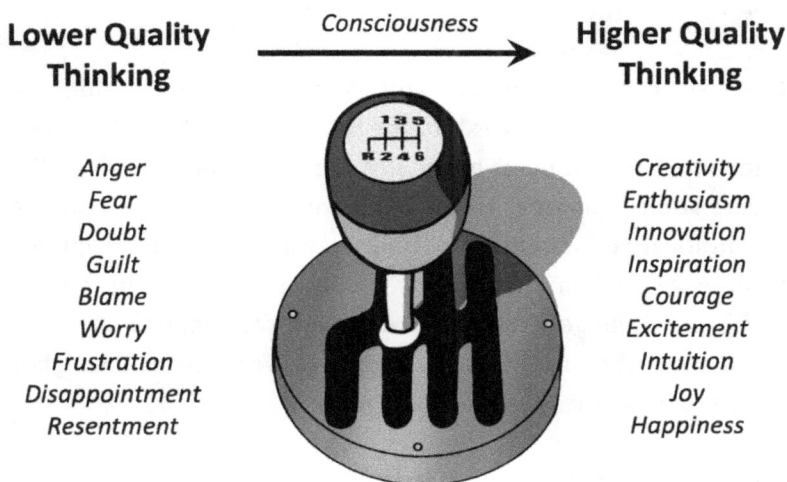

Lower Quality Thinking — *Consciousness* → **Higher Quality Thinking**

Lower Quality Thinking	Higher Quality Thinking
Anger	Creativity
Fear	Enthusiasm
Doubt	Innovation
Guilt	Inspiration
Blame	Courage
Worry	Excitement
Frustration	Intuition
Disappointment	Joy
Resentment	Happiness

Figure 2. The Gearbox

Imagine that the human mind is a gearbox in a car with manual transmission. (Rare these days, I know!) There are multiple gears in addition to the neutral and reverse positions.

We, the driver of our mind, can choose to set our gearbox to neutral. Nothing much happens there for us on an emotional level. We don't make any judgments about what's happening; we fully accept things as they are and life goes on.

We can also find ourselves in reverse gear, which makes it impossible to make progress. When we go into reverse gear, our quality of thinking drops and our mind fills with thoughts that put us in a bad mood. This can involve judging people or ideas, making assumptions, or misinterpreting situations happening in the world around us. We perceive some sort of threat, which puts our nervous system in fight-or-flight mode, which in turn creates feelings of fear, insecurity, anger, frustration, discouragement, stress, or concern. We see limited or no options, complain, criticize, or withdraw from the situation completely.

Once we shift into gears one and above, our quality of thinking increases. The higher we shift, the better it gets. As we train our minds to function more optimally, our consciousness rises. We access additional areas of the brain, resulting in more creative and innovative thoughts. We feel increasingly grateful, compassionate, excited, and confident. We also experience more trust and joy. In high gear, we're more productive, make better decisions, and feel more alive and connected. We perform at a higher level and make progress more quickly.

All day inside our heads, we switch gears as we go through life. Rather than operating on autopilot, we can choose to move up or down in the spectrum of thoughts and emotions at any moment according to what the situation we're in calls for. When we're conscious of our gearbox, we remain aware of the fact that our thoughts determine our feelings and actions.

To translate this awareness of our mind into effective leadership, we have to examine the way we feel. Our feelings serve as indicators of our subjective level of thinking in the present moment. Although our feelings aren't directly *caused* by external circumstances, they help us understand how we *perceive* those circumstances.

When you interact with people operating in reverse mode, perhaps withdrawing or expressing frustration, what you're seeing is their perception of the situation from a low level of thinking. Responding to them calmly and listening with compassion, openness, and curiosity will give you a better understanding of how they view what's happening.

When you find yourself in reverse mode, realize that your decisions, productivity, and communication with others will be of low quality, making your leadership less effective overall. Remind yourself that *you don't have to believe your own thoughts.* We often assume that because our thoughts appear in our heads, they must therefore all be true. That's not the case, but the more attention we give our thoughts, the more we believe them. If those thoughts are negative, we're likely to give them inordinate amounts of time and attention, causing them to stick around even longer.

Over time, the beliefs we regularly reinforce create a story that determines our emotions and behavior. For this reason, we have to be careful with our negative thoughts. They can feel deeply important but are still just thoughts like any other. If we can notice them without giving them much heed, or switch into a different gear in our mind, they'll eventually disappear.

The Power of Shifting Gears

I've witnessed the transformational power of shifting gears many times while working with my clients. One woman I used to coach, who held a senior role at a large international bank in Asia, hopped onto one of our calls desperate to talk about a litany of changes happening at her company.

A new CEO had recently been appointed. The first thing he did was fire her boss, who she had aligned well with on values and leadership style. The man she'd worked with for years was suddenly gone and wouldn't be replaced. She had no way of knowing what this change would mean for her and her team. They were stressed, working without an anchor to plan around.

My client was scheduled to meet with the new CEO the day after our call and wasn't sure what to expect. She didn't know how to prepare for their upcoming conversation. It didn't surprise me that she was having so much trouble getting ready for the meeting. Stress had sent her tumbling down a rabbit hole of unproductive thoughts to the point where she could no longer think clearly. She was focusing so hard on the situation with her new CEO, which she viewed as the problem at hand, that she lost the ability to see the forest for the trees. Her external circumstances weren't the problem. It was her own thinking surrounding her fear of what was happening that was causing her distress.

At this point in the conversation, my client and I began brainstorming other perspectives that were available to her. I asked her what she thought the three biggest challenges for her new CEO might be. As she thought about the question, her feelings shifted. She was no longer focused on herself, her situation, and all the stress plaguing *her*. She answered by saying he would need to understand the organization better. He would also want to make an impact quickly, and therefore need to act quickly. We began brainstorming ways she and her team could assist him with those goals. How could she help her new CEO?

The next day, she walked into her meeting with a list of topics to discuss. She talked about the people on her team who could help her new CEO map out the organization and identify important stakeholders. Shifting her thinking had given her the ability to view the possibilities in front of her with greater clarity. She was no longer driving in reverse, fixated on her negative view and the fear it was causing for her and her team. Instead, she shifted into a higher gear and got creative about ideas she and her CEO could explore together.

As a species, we're designed to operate in neutral or above. Joy is our natural state. Fear is the exception rather than the norm—a defense mechanism that kicks in to help us survive. It's in our nature to make progress rather than getting stuck in reverse. By mastering your own gearbox, you'll be able to remain in your optimal mode of operation regardless of what's happening around you.

How to Shift into High Gear

With more self-awareness, you can intentionally raise your quality of thinking in the moment. You can start leveling up in all aspects of leadership represented by the rings in Figure 1 by viewing your thoughts and feelings as sources of enormously valuable information. If you can begin recognizing the patterns your thoughts, emotions, and actions tend to follow, you can manage them in ways that work for you rather than against you. Here are seven exercises to help you shift into a higher gear.

1. Observe your thoughts.

Remember: just because a thought pops up in your head doesn't make it true or intrinsic to who you are. You are not your thoughts. Instead of personalizing them, just observe them without judgment. Try writing them down for even greater clarity.

What you'll realize, first of all, is that there's an awful lot of thinking happening in your head at any given time. You'll also begin to understand what self-awareness really feels like. Humans are the only species capable of observing our own thinking. That's quite unique.

Eventually, you'll become more cognizant of your thought patterns. How much time do you spend in neutral mode? How about in reverse? How about the higher gears? How do you feel while you're thinking particular thoughts? When you're in reverse and upset about something, what sensations are created in your body?

2. Become aware of your triggers.

When we're emotionally triggered, we're more likely to shift into reverse gear and react (rather than consciously respond) to situations. Recognize which thoughts and feelings cause you to switch to a lower gear. Recognize your feelings don't stem from what someone else has said, but from your thoughts about what they expressed.

Anytime you feel strong emotions coming on in the workplace, ask yourself what's truly making you upset.

Fill in the blanks below based on what you tend to experience:

- "I get angry when _____."

- "I can't stand it when people _____."

- "I feel disappointed when _____."

- "I get anxious when _____."

- "I feel insecure when _____."

- "I feel frustrated when _____."

Again, no one can *make* you feel anything. Your unique interpretation of what's happening is what's causing your unpleasant emotions. Once you understand this, you can begin to weigh other interpretations of the situation that might be more accurate.

It's also helpful to consider the positive emotions that lie at the other end of the spectrum. What triggers you to feel excited, peaceful, satisfied, inspired, confident, fulfilled, or joyful? What's at the core of *those* emotions and how can you create more of them?

I once worked with a management consultant who had led many complex digital transformation processes for large organizations. He prides himself on his wealth of knowledge and has never stopped learning over the course of his career. He recently got upset when one of his prospects didn't accept a proposal he had put a lot of work into preparing. He was quick to judge the other party. "They just don't get it, and I can't work with people who can't meet my standards." When we talked about the situation, it turned out there was no evidence that this company lacked respect for his ideas. There may have been a hundred different reasons for their rejection of his proposal. It was my client's *interpretation* that the rejection was about him.

Our human tendency to mentally position ourselves at the center of the universe often prevents us from seeing the objective reality of whatever we're dealing with. Rather than seeking *the* truth, we jump to unfounded conclusions and become blinded by *our* truth. I'm not suggesting, of course, that you ignore your intuition or disregard your own perspective. What I'm suggesting is that you slow down and take the time to evaluate an array of possibilities before drawing your conclusions. Understand what might actually be happening so you can *respond* rather than *react*.

When we knock ourselves out of emotional autopilot, we begin to express ourselves totally differently in our interactions with others. We gain the ability to get truly curious about why the people we work with behave in the ways they do. We stop automatically judging them as incapable or unwilling. There may be any number of explanations at any given time that may have nothing to do with us whatsoever. Don't let your triggers take the wheel.

3. Stop believing your thoughts.

Make a habit of questioning your thoughts. "What story am I making up about what's happening and how close to the truth is it?" Before reacting, explore other ways of viewing the situation. Then, *choose* how you want to show up and respond mindfully.

Like many professionals, you may find yourself wrestling with imposter syndrome. This is the little voice in your head that's always questioning you; it tells you you're not good enough, not qualified enough, or not experienced enough. It may try to convince you that you've only made it this far due to luck. Someday people will find out you're not actually as good as everyone believes.

This judgmental voice is rooted in fear, not reality. It fears change and wants to prevent you from growing. Don't believe its lies. There's no life-threatening danger waiting behind the next corner, no matter how hard your thoughts and emotions try to convince you to stay put.

The most common fears I see leaders struggle with:

- Not being good enough to succeed

- Failure or poor performance

- Being unworthy of success

- Embarrassment

- Change or the unknown

- Making mistakes

- Losing someone or something they hold dear

- Losing their power or influence

- Losing their skills as they age

Few people will actually articulate their subconscious fears. More often, they'll behave in certain ways to avoid confronting them.

The most common behaviors of fear avoidance:

- Procrastination

- Ignoring problems

- Controlling behaviors

- People pleasing

- Perfectionism

- Hyper-achievement

When you find yourself locked in a fear spiral, stop and notice that your imposter syndrome is playing mind games again. The fear itself is not real. Change the story you're telling yourself. Choose who you want to be in the new story. What would it look like if you were the most amazing leader you could possibly be? Start showing up from that place.

4. Discuss your thoughts with someone else.

When you're in a senior leadership role, you'll likely have very few people around you who feel comfortable giving you honest feedback. The higher up you move within an organization, the quieter your coworkers will get regarding how you can improve. As the pool of people you can rely on for advice and feedback shrinks, how can you ensure you continue to grow?

I advise all executives to surround themselves with at least a handful of people who are willing to give them honest feedback. Get specific. Ask them for reflections and recommendations about particular ideas you've shared, beliefs you're expressing, or ways you've communicated. Ask for their opinions on how they think you can do better. You don't have to agree with what they tell you or follow their advice, but you'll at least gain insight into how others are experiencing you. You could hire a coach. As is the case in sports, the better you get, the more you'll benefit from support that helps you perform at your best.

5. Turn your attention to helping others.

When we're in reverse gear, helping others can be a great way to get out of our own heads. At work, this can center on serving the people in your team, having conversations to offer support, or asking others what you can do to make their job easier. Get creative, and you'll find yourself more focused on solutions than problems.

6. Practice gratitude.

It's impossible to remain in reverse or even neutral gear while practicing gratitude. The moment we start focusing on what we're grateful for, our mind immediately instructs our body to create positive feelings.

What are you happy about at work? There's always *something* to be grateful for. The next time you find yourself in low gear, think of three things big or small that you can appreciate about your current situation. Gratitude is an easy and effective antidote to fear and frustration, and it's available to you instantly, at all times.

7. Keep a "Mind Matters" journal.

Another way to exercise your self-awareness muscles is to make a daily habit of journaling about your experiences. Putting your thoughts down on paper will help you get them out of your head where you can see them. Then you can reflect upon them, notice patterns in your perception, and figure out what to do next.

It's far easier to analyze our thoughts and feelings once they're outside of us. Ultimately, journaling can free up loads more mental bandwidth than we're used to having. You'll be able to move on from thoughts that have been gnawing at your mind, keeping you stuck in emotions that aren't serving you.

So far, we've talked about how your thoughts, feelings, and actions determine your beliefs and perspectives. Next, we'll create clarity around your purpose, values, and leadership skills.

2

YOUR PURPOSE, VALUES, AND LEADERSHIP SKILLS

Your Anchor, Compass, and Approach

"Often leaders have the best intentions, but people cannot read their minds. That's why it's important to declare yourself; Tell people why you choose to lead and the code you live by."

—DOUGLAS CONANT

LET'S TAKE ANOTHER LOOK AT OUR JOURNEY THROUGH THE inner rings of the Core Leadership Methodology illustration.

So far, we've covered how you can optimize your thoughts, feelings, and actions, which determine your beliefs and perspectives. We'll now continue our journey through the second and third rings to examine your purpose, values, and leadership skills.

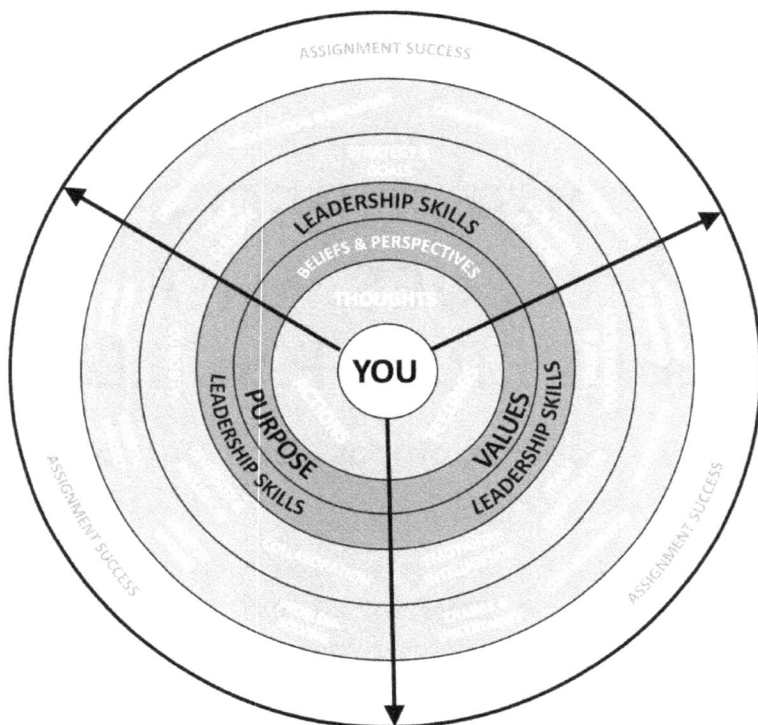

Figure 1.2 Core Leadership Methodology

STATEMENT OF COMMITMENT AND KNOWING YOUR PURPOSE

With everything you'll encounter in your first 100 days and beyond, understanding *why* you accepted your new mission in the first place is essential. Defining this will help you be intentional about *how* you're going to embark on this journey and the specifics of what you're committing yourself to.

Start by taking some time to answer the following three questions:

1. Why have you taken on this role, and what are you committing yourself to over the next 100 days?

2. If you were to call me two years from now and say, "Liesbeth, these two years have been the most successful and fulfilling of my life," what would you be telling me? Within that vision, describe the following in the present tense:

   a. What your personal and professional life both look like

   b. What it feels like now that you achieved what you were aiming for

   c. The things you've accomplished in the last two years that made an impact

   d. How you're showing up as a leader on a day-to-day basis

3. If, say, you didn't end up achieving the results you were aiming for, what role would you have played in that outcome?

Having clarity on why you accepted your role, why this opportunity excites you, and exactly what you're aiming to accomplish will provide you with an anchor to ground you when the going gets tough. It will help remind you to stay on target and keep moving forward regardless of what's happening at the time. Absorbing what it will feel like to succeed will keep your fire and vision alive.

YOUR PERSONAL VALUES: THE COMPASS GUIDING YOUR WAY

What are values, exactly? Essentially, they're the principles you live by. I like to think of values as our personal nonnegotiables. They're the aspects of our life we're unwilling to compromise on, which makes them hugely influential in guiding our decisions. On a subconscious level, our values tell us whether or not our lives are turning out how we would like them to.

When our values are being honored, we feel happy, fulfilled, and successful. We live with a sense of lightness that tells us we're on the right track. When our values are being challenged or compromised, we may experience any number of different sensations, like anger, frustration, disappointment, or a sense of emptiness or numbness. We can use our feelings as signals that tell us whether we're living in alignment with the person we want to be and if not, make the necessary changes.

Years ago, I coached a man named Jared who worked for an international tech company. He was successful, likable, and easy to get along with. He came to me because he felt like he was letting the people he worked with down. He had too much on his plate and lacked the time and energy to properly help any of them. He felt overwhelmed, frustrated, and disappointed in himself for failing to finish his projects within the desired time frame. He also feared for his health. There was a history of heart failure in his family, and he worried that if he didn't get his stress under control, he'd be forging a difficult path for his future.

While talking with Jared, I noticed how hard it seemed to be for him to say no to other people. He wanted to please everyone, even to the detriment of his own health. When we can't say no, we can't get our priorities in order and end up failing to give proper attention to anything we do. That's when we began to do value work in our sessions. It was clear that staying healthy was immensely important to Jared and he was compromising his ability to do so for the sake of his job.

For Jared, the cost of going against his values was too high. As we worked together, he focused on learning to set healthy boundaries around his health and his work. When people asked him for a favor that went outside his boundaries, he told them he appreciated the request, but had made a commitment to himself to focus on his health and would have to decline. This ended up making people respect him *more,* creating the opposite result of the fear he'd been harboring. He was also able to zero in on the tasks and projects he wanted to prioritize at work, based on what energized rather than drained him.

With the time he'd freed up outside of work, Jared got back into inline skating, which he had loved when he was younger. His health improved and six months later, he got in touch to say he was taking part in an international inline skating championship competition. Through the act of putting boundaries in place around his values, Jared cleared the way for changes that allowed him to live the life he'd been wanting.

Value work is essential to leadership success. You can kickstart this process by completing the following value exercise.

Identifying Your Personal Core Values

1. Select the values on the list below that resonate with you most, words that represent what you care about most, or the ideas you live by. Pick out no more than ten.

Abundance	Courage	Independence	Professionalism
Acceptance	Creativity	Inner Peace	Recognition
Accomplishment	Determination	Innovation	Resilience
Accuracy	Diversity	Integrity	Respect
Achievement	Education	Intelligence	Responsibility
Adventure	Efficiency	Intimacy	Safety
Altruism	Environment	Joy	Security
Authenticity	Equality	Justice	Self-Awareness
Autonomy	Excellence	Leadership	Self-Confidence
Balance	Fairness	Learning	Self-Expression
Beauty	Family	Longevity	Service
Calmness	Freedom	Love	Spirituality
Challenge	Friendship	Loyalty	Structure
Clarity	Fulfillment	Modesty	Talent
Collaboration	Fun	Nature	Tradition
Commitment	Growth Mindset	Open Mindedness	Trust
Communication	Happiness	Passion	Truth
Community	Health	Patience	Vision
Competition	Honesty	Personal Growth	Vitality
Compliance	Humor	Positivity	Walking the Talk
Connecting to Others	Imagination	Power	Wealth
Consistency	Inclusiveness	Privacy	Wisdom

2. Trim your selection down to a maximum of five core values. Which do you care about most? You can group similar-sounding values and choose one label that covers them all. Take out those that are less important to you.

3. Now prioritize them in order of importance.

4. Reflect on your five core values and ask yourself:

   - How do I act on these core values in my life?

   - In what areas of my life can I express myself more according to my core values?

   - In what areas of my life do I *not* express myself according to my core values at all?

   - What would be the benefits of expressing myself in ways that align better with my values?

   - What's preventing me from expressing myself in ways that align better with my values?

   - What might be a sign that my behavior is not aligned with my values?

   - How can I better incorporate my core values into my leadership role?

   - When I feel triggered, which of my values is being undermined?

   - How can I use my values in decision-making?

   - How do my values affect my leadership performance?

By taking the time to define and reflect on your values, you'll gain a clearer sense of what motivates and drives you in life. You'll be able to map out the changes you need to make on your path to greater ease, contentment, and fulfillment. You'll also collect valuable information you can then use to determine your priorities, make fruitful decisions, and set meaningful goals.

It's important to note the fact that everyone in the world, whether they're conscious of them or not, has core values that have been formed according to their unique life experiences. You'll sometimes encounter people whose core values conflict with yours, sometimes drastically, which can explain why you feel more comfortable with some people than others.

In cultures that are foreign to you, people are bound to have values that differ from yours. We have to be careful not to make any judgments here. There's no reason to believe our values are superior to those of anyone else. Value clashes are often at the core of conflict, but instead of arguing, defending your values, or trying to convince others to deprioritize their own, realize they simply have different principles motivating their behavior. It's not personal, it's just human nature.

Three Strategies to Choose from When Values Clash

1. **Ignore:** Sometimes a conflict of values amounts to a small, insignificant issue that's not relevant enough to be worth addressing. Let's say one of your core values is punctuality, and someone submits a report to you an hour later than agreed. If no one seems concerned and no major consequences ensue, you may just want to ignore it.

2. **Discuss:** If you notice certain decisions or actions are happening consistently and undermining your values or those of the company, you may want to address this. If so, bring up the issue in a kind and respectful way to see if it can be resolved. People may not be conscious of what's happening and making a simple analogy may be enough to bring their attention to it.

3. **Negotiate:** If a clash of values involves multiple people or the situation becomes complex, more negotiation will be needed. There may be no easy answers to the issue. In such cases, it's even more important to remain nonjudgmental. Stay focused on the problem, not the person. It may take a bit more time to come up with creative solutions. Start by asking these questions:

   a. What are the elements you can agree on?

   b. What are the possible solutions that best align with the company's values?

   c. What are some ways forward based on the common goals and interests of those involved?

   d. How can the answers to these questions be used as a basis for cooperative collaboration?

The best way forward in all situations involving value clashes is to focus on points of commonality. I'll revisit the specifics of this topic several times throughout the course of this book.

ASSESS YOUR LEADERSHIP SKILLS

Now that we've discussed your values, we're going to move outward to the next ring of the Core Leadership Methodology illustration: your leadership skills.

Being successful in your new role will depend on the professional skills and knowledge needed to effectively interact with your team and company stakeholders. You have to know what your strengths are and how to leverage them to your benefit. It's also helpful to become mindful of the gaps in your knowledge and identify the degree to which the skills you lack will be needed in your new role.

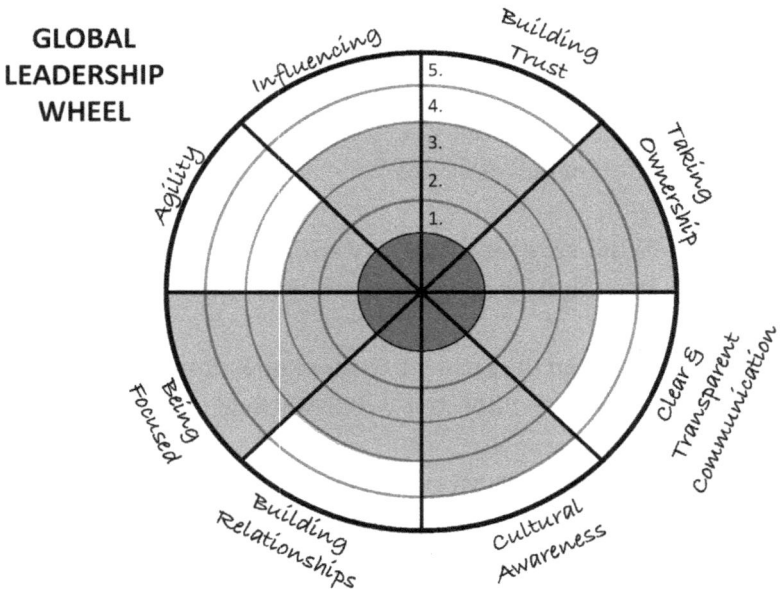

Figure 4. The Global Leadership Wheel

While doing research for this book, I asked leaders what they believed to be the most valuable leadership skills for people in global roles. I've narrowed down their top eight answers.

Building Trust

At the top on the right, I start with the skill of building trust. This is about how you connect, listen, and talk with others in order to build what I call professional intimacy. In these relationships, conversations don't revolve solely around work. Instead, you pay an honest interest in who others are at the human level. What do they like? What's their situation at home? What do they enjoy doing outside of work? You find out what's important to them and what drives them.

If we want professional intimacy to form, we can't expect others to share their stories unless we're willing to share ours as well. We can model this through our actions. We have to create an environment of psychological safety that invites everyone to feel vulnerable enough to share mistakes as well as triumphs. An environment where people feel supported by you and their other team members. A team that knows you'll have their back when they need it, and where you know they'll do the same for you. We'll cover this as part of the Connect, Inspire, Grow framework over the next few chapters.

Taking Ownership

Taking ownership is about fully committing to your goals, maximizing resilience, and remaining determined to push through when things get tough throughout your assignment. As the leader of your project, you're responsible for the process and outcome of your team's actions. I've spoken with many people who felt frustrated and overwhelmed at some point. This is a natural, unavoidable part of the process.

Taking ownership gives you the ability to respond (rather than react) to whatever comes your way, knowing you'll only make it through the challenges you face if you accept full responsibility for every step of the process. This entails taking ownership of your mindset, decisions, priorities, and actions.

Clear and Transparent Communication

As a global leader, you work in an environment involving a large diversity of people. Additionally, you're likely to work with many people for whom English is a second, third, or even fourth language, which makes clarity in communication essential. Be mindful not to speak or write using too much region-specific jargon, slang, idioms, or tricky words that may be too nuanced or difficult to understand. Keep your messages to your team short, concise, and intentional.

Transparency is all about sharing both good and bad information in a way that clearly conveys the "why" behind the message. Share important news with the team when you get it, even when you don't have all the answers yet. Be clear about what they can and can't share outside of the team or organization and why.

- "Here's why we're changing this policy."

- "Let me tell you why our team is in this situation."

- "Here's why we're not sharing this information now."

Cultural Awareness

You'll have an easier transition and become effective in your role more quickly if you approach your new environment with a sense of curiosity. Open-mindedness toward other cultural identities is essential. This involves recognizing, understanding, and respecting that we all have different values, which were influenced by our diverse backgrounds and experiences. If you're open to learning about new and wildly different ways of working, you'll have a far easier time connecting with people. (Specific challenges regarding culture are covered in Chapter 6, so stay tuned.)

Building Relationships

Being successful in your role will require you to develop and maintain healthy relationships both inside and outside your organization. You'll need these relationships to be strong if you're going to influence others and achieve common goals.

Being Focused

In 1971, Nobel Prize-winning economist Herbert Simon said, "Wealth of information creates poverty of attention." With this quote, he pointed out a direct link between high performance and the ability to focus. What's your level of skill when it comes to allocating your attention in an environment with an over-abundance of stimuli?

Stepping into a new role in a foreign country can be chaotic and full of distractions. You'll regularly encounter situations you don't completely understand. It can feel very overwhelming. You've got to be able to stay focused on the task at hand, one step at a time, to get where you want to be.

If you're someone who is easily distracted, this can be challenging. When you're not able to think clearly and channel your energy into what you need to accomplish, there's no room for creativity. Every distraction will have the power to rob you of your mental bandwidth and cause you to waste time on concerns that don't matter. In the long run, this has the potential to slow your productivity down and hurt your credibility.

Agility

Agility requires us to stop, reset, and change direction when situations change. The business world is typically volatile, but working in an environment you don't fully understand is bound to increase its volatility for you. You won't have all the information about what's happening, especially at the beginning of your assignment. You may have to depend on secondhand information that's been translated for you. You might only understand bits and pieces of the full picture. You might struggle deeply with language barriers. In all of these situations, you'll have to think on your feet and adapt.

Don't be afraid to admit when you've judged a situation inaccurately and want to change your mind. Be open and transparent with others about your thought process and aim for the best solution rather than *your* solution to a problem. Learn to be comfortable in ambiguity.

Influencing

Effective leaders focus on **how they show up** and **are intentional** about **what they can do or say to convey a message** that **inspires others to accomplish an outcome**.

Let's break this down:

- **How do you show up?** Bring your authentic self to every interaction and generate positive energy that attracts people. High energy attracts high energy.

- **What's your intention?** Realize that every situation is an opportunity for you to bring the conversation to a higher level.

- **What's the roadmap to the future?** Create a bold and compelling vision and provide clarity around how you intend to co-create that future with the people involved.

- **WIIFT: What's in it for them?** Understand that influencing people starts with "serving" them. It has little to do with "convincing" them, or worse, striving for power over them.

Have clarity about who will be impacted by your plans and work to build relationships with them. If you know what they're trying to achieve, help them first. Provide value to them to build credibility and trust. They'll then be willing to give back to invest in the relationship and help you achieve what you want. It's a process of give and take, but the giving must come from you first.

Now that you've read about each skill on the Global Leadership Wheel, rank your level of proficiency in each area. The higher the number you choose, the more confident you feel with that skill. As you assess yourself in each of these areas, think about the following questions.

- "What are my strengths in this area, and how can I capitalize on them?"

- "Where are there gaps?"

- "How important is this skill for success in my new role?"

- "How important is it for me to have that skill for my team or the organization to be successful?"

By assessing the current state of your skills, you'll be able to build on your strengths and create a strategy to fill the gaps through additional leadership development areas like, for instance, training, coaching, or mentoring.

Below you'll find additional aspects of senior leadership. Use them to identify which qualities are important for you in your new role, and you rate yourself on them on a scale from 1-5.

LEADERSHIP SKILL	RATING	LEADERSHIP SKILL	RATING
Accountability		Humor	
Achieving Sustainable Results		Innovative Thinking	
Acknowledging and Praising		Inspiring Others	
Approachability		Integrity	
Business Acumen		Managing Diversity	
Change Management		Mentoring	
Charisma		Negotiating	
Commitment		Networking	
Conflict Management		Patience	
Credibility		People Development	
Dealing with Uncertainty		Perseverance	
Emotional Intelligence		Planning and Organizing	
Excellence		Prioritizing	
Execution		Problem Solving	
Experience		Productivity	
Experimenting		Reliability	
Fostering Talent		Respect	
Giving Feedback		Risk Management	
Goal Setting		Storytelling	
Handling Criticism		Strategic Thinking	
Healthy Debate		Technological Knowledge	

So far in this book, we've covered how you can prepare to lead others by learning to lead yourself before your assignment has even begun. Next, I'll talk about the Connect, Inspire, Grow framework itself, which consists of best practices for navigating the three phases leaders go through when they start a new role. How can you use your first 100 days to create a foundation for success that will serve you and your team throughout your assignment?

During your first 40 days, your time will be best spent focusing on connecting with those you'll be leading. What does that process look like? Who will be in those initial meetings and what will you discuss with them?

Between days 40 to 80, how can you consolidate the information you've collected, channel it into the mission ahead of you, and prepare your team for what's next? How can you inspire the people on your team to buy into your vision and get fully on board?

From day 80 onward, how can you ensure that by the end of your contract you've not only completed your mission, but grown your team members into leaders who can continue to thrive long after you've left?

The answers to these questions and more lie ahead in Part 2.

PART 2

A FRAMEWORK FOR THE FIRST 100 DAYS

3

CONNECT
The First 40 Days

"Don't talk to the mask. Talk to the soul behind the mask, and eventually that's who'll talk back to you."

—DR. BILL PETTIT

ANY BUSINESS WE DO IS ROOTED IN RELATIONSHIPS. OUR WORK on a project always boils down to the people who are involved, what they bring to the table, and how they collaborate. Relationships are the most important thing we need to work on if we're to excel at leadership and succeed in our assignments.

As leaders, we have to focus on people over tasks. During the first forty days of your role, try to answer the question of *who* you're going to meet with rather than *what* you need to do. Keep in mind that building relationships with your people should be your priority; the best place you can direct your focus from day one is the building of trust.

There's a wealth of evidence suggesting that leaders who take the time to build trust ultimately see results more quickly because their teams end up performing better. They become more productive and innovative, but more importantly, happier and more loyal. Those last two elements are crucial, as they're often lacking within companies that have trouble engaging and retaining talent. In a 2019 *Harvard Business Review* piece titled "How Leaders Around the World Build Trust Across Cultures," authors Mansour Javidan and Aks Zaheer concluded that when individuals trust one another, they can work together effectively regardless of cultural differences. When you dig deep and connect with one another at the human level, beyond work-related conversations, you can tap into the essence of what unites us all. Once you've made it there, it won't matter where the people you lead were born or raised.

In this chapter, I'll talk about how you can connect with your new team members on a deeper, more personal level that establishes a solid foundation of trust. You'll learn who you should be meeting with during your first meetings and how to use that time effectively. But first, let's start by exploring the three levels of relationship commonly present within modern organizations.

THE THREE LEVELS OF RELATIONSHIP

The nature of our relationships with our team members, stakeholders, and other colleagues are likely to fall into one of three categories.

The Transactional Level

The lowest level of relationship in the workplace exists at the transactional level, which revolves solely around task and reward, which comes in the form of remuneration. Employees are asked to carry out tasks according to their job description and receive their paycheck in exchange at the end of the pay period. Building mutual trust and loyalty is of little to no concern in these cases, which means that when one of the two factors of the equation changes—namely, when conditions regarding remuneration change or their job description is modified—people rethink their options and may decide to leave.

I've heard leaders complain on many occasions about losing talent at their organization because those team members can earn a bit more money somewhere else. They complain about a lack of loyalty and feel discouraged that pay seems to be the only driving factor for those they hire. I challenge them to explore the "need" behind their employees' desire to earn more that's not currently being addressed.

A PwC survey of 1,800 Australian workers in 2021 revealed that 38 percent were thinking about leaving their employer within the following twelve months. Global rates were expected to be higher. A second PwC analysis showed that globally, the relative importance of financial compensation had declined by 11 percent over the past decade. The importance of other types of benefits—medical, dental, vision and life insurance, wellness, and supplemental health benefits like childcare—had doubled. Work-life balance options and training and career development have tripled in importance. The pandemic shifted employees' priorities and what they find important (in terms of how they spend their time and money) even more. We neglect to take this into account when we solely look at *wages* and *tasks*.

I recently spoke to a head of corporate banking for a global bank with branches all over the world. He had worked in Europe, the US, the Middle East, Africa, and extensively in Asia. Eventually, he was transferred to a position in London and ran into problems with the new team assigned to him. Due to increased regulations and legal sanctions, his bank, along with many others, suddenly experienced an influx of administrative work that had to be done if the company was to remain compliant.

This work became a major burden for the junior members of his team. They wanted to problem solve and handle complex transactions, not get bogged down in admin tasks. His challenge was to keep them motivated in order not to lose them in the long run. The organization boosted salaries and bonuses enormously, but the junior staff weren't looking for financial incentives.

If the reward for employees revolves solely around money or benefits, they'll have no reason not to move on when a more lucrative opportunity presents itself. Highly talented people rarely stay with organizations that don't make the most of the skills they offer.

The Strategic Level

The second level of relationship revolves around strategies that focus mainly on performance and outcome. In these cases, leaders attempt to build high-performing teams, but often fail because their organizations operate according to fixed constructs like traditional career paths and strict hierarchy across roles. The company can appear to be doing everything right, offering employees flexibility, good benefits, and attractive payment packages. They've defined their company values, but those values aren't subsequently translated through desirable leadership behavior. Performance is only measured by financial results. There's no reward for people to drive trust-building elements like collaboration, shared goals, and open communication. Due to the lack of collaboration and a shared team culture, people don't work from a place of connection and trust, but stay focused on achieving individual financial targets, so silos remain intact.

In cases like these, open communication becomes impossible. Sometimes there are unwritten rules about who can connect with whom. Employees don't have the freedom to approach colleagues at other levels of the organization's hierarchy to solve problems. (At least, not until they're promoted to the same level.) They have no means of collaborating while working to accomplish shared goals. There's little transparency and flow of information from the top down, so there's also no flow of ideas or innovation from the bottom up. In the end, progress is slow and people work for their own benefit, not the team's or the company's. Therefore, outcomes end up less than ideal.

I recently saw an example of this play out with a client of mine who worked as a partner at a consulting firm in Hong Kong. She had worked hard for many years to climb the traditional company career ladder and finally arrived at the top and earned the role of partner in the firm, where she had always aspired to be. In spite of her esteemed position, she felt frustrated by the fact that the different teams of the company were working in silos. The other partners she worked with did everything they could to minimize the amount of people involved in their projects. They wanted to avoid dividing the eventual bonus they'd earn from their client's fee among too many parties. While working within this construct, they were unable to collaborate with people who would have been an enormous asset had they been invited to the table. This strategy, which was aimed at garnering maximum profit, ended up hindering the potential of the individuals and teams as a whole.

The Human Level

The final level of relationship in the workplace is the human level, which is where we aim to arrive in this book. Here, we experience a deeper connection with our team members that goes beyond task, reward, and even culture. This type of connection lays the groundwork for professional intimacy, which we touched on in the last chapter. The dynamic is such that we know what the people we work with desire, what their needs are, what drives them, and what they value. It's a process of getting to know people for who they truly are.

Three Universal Human Desires

1. People want to be **seen**. We must aim to pay a sincere interest in their opinions and views and create an environment where they can fully express themselves without the fear of judgment.

2. People want to be **respected**. As their leader, we need to ensure that we recognize others' contributions, allow people to take ownership of projects, involve them in decision-making, and show appreciation.

3. People want to **grow**, whatever growth looks like for *them*. That could relate to monetary or personal growth. It could involve acquiring new knowledge or learning new skills. People seek some kind of increase, expansion, or advancement in their lives. We have to give them the chance to expand or advance in the specific ways they desire if we're to form human-level relationships with them. Otherwise, they're likely to look elsewhere eventually.

I was recently talking with a client, a financial executive working in Shanghai. In the past, he had worked positions in a number of locations in and outside the US and prided himself on his relationship-building skills. When he spoke with me, however, he was running into conflict with a woman he had hired a few months before. While he did everything he could to open doors for her and make her landing within the organization a smooth one, during one meeting, she exploded at him. She began crying and shouting at him for not listening to her, getting too involved in her work, and being overbearing. He was shocked not only by what felt like a personal attack on him, but by the fact that he hadn't seen this coming.

"How could I have missed whatever the problem was before it got to this point?"

As it turned out, my client's new employee hadn't been feeling seen or respected. When she got hired, he had gone into problem-solving mode, introducing her to important people, getting them to warm up to her, and going out of his way to pave the way for her to build connections. That's not what *she* wanted, however. From her perspective, she was a professional and wanted to take those steps herself. She felt as if he was undermining her experience and behaving condescendingly by forming her working relationships for her.

Once he and I had identified where he had misaligned with her needs, he called her into a feedback session that ended up being immensely productive. They discussed their personal motivators, aspirations, and more. By the end of the conversation, he understood what she wanted and needed. He was then able to align with her professionally in a way that suited her as an individual rather than taking an approach that he envisioned to be the right one.

As team leaders, it's our responsibility to meet every member of our team on the human level. We don't have to facilitate their whole lives, but having a sense of what's important to them, how they want to grow, and what kind of flexibility they might need can make or break their experience at work. The only way they will open up, show themselves, and share their needs and desires is if they're able to connect with someone who is genuinely interested in *who* they are and *what* drives them. They have to feel you'll be able to help them advance in their careers. I thoroughly believe, and have heard many leaders confirm, that connecting on this level is the key component of retaining the talent modern organizations need to thrive.

PREPARING TO CONNECT

As you prepare for your initial meetings, start by identifying who you need to connect with during the first several weeks of your assignment. You can move all around the company meeting people and getting to know them, but as we know, your time is limited. It's therefore crucial to zero in on the specific people you need to build relationships with in order to accomplish your mission.

Traditional onboarding programs typically set us up to meet with certain colleagues according to existing organizational structures. Apart from familiarizing you with the company's policies and protocols, HR or your manager will schedule meetings for you with executive teams, the board of directors, colleagues, and team members. This may also involve conversations with people they believe can give you a fuller perspective.

To build the right connections more quickly, however, I recommend implementing a strategy I call capability-based networking. Rather than connecting with people you assume you're supposed to talk with, create your new network based on the *capabilities* and *knowledge* you need in order to achieve the goals of your assignment. Seek out the people who have what you need. Figure out exactly how they can help you. The people you form your network with should fill in the answers to all your "who" questions.

- *Who has the know-how I need?*

- *Who will be impacted by the work I'll be doing?*

- *Who are the company's main influencers?*

- *Who can I go to for support?*

Leaders often tend to only look for know-how within their own region, division, functional area, or line of authority. Broadening that scope will give you a "bigger pond to fish in" in terms of geography, culture, functions, clients, or essential players in the market. You cannot be an expert in everything. Have self-awareness as to what your expertise is and be honest and clear about where the gaps are. Who can supplement that knowledge? By getting those answers from the organization early on, you'll spend your time more efficiently and be able to focus on the knowledge, skills, and solutions you need for your assignment more quickly.

Denise, a Dutch business executive at Bank of America in Hong Kong, relayed to me how important it is to meet with the right people at the beginning of a new assignment. When she first arrived there, she made the mistake of trying to connect with as many people as possible rather than the specific people she needed to work with. She wasn't entirely clear on what she needed to accomplish her mission and ended up wasting a lot of time talking with people who weren't relevant to her project. This slowed her down in ways she went on to regret, but she learned an important lesson about preparing mindfully for those initial conversations in the future.

The Connect Card

The Connect Card is a tool that will help you build connections with the right people before your assignment has begun.

CONNECT CARD

Project Vision:

Project Goal:

Purpose:
-
-
-

Impact:
-
-
-

Success Indicators:
-
-
-
-
-
-
-
-
-

Outcome:
-
-
-

Know-how:
-
-
-

Influencers:
-
-
-

CONNECT CARD

Project Vision:
Describe the grand idea of where the team or project is going. The aim of the project vision is to guide, motivate, and inspire the people who are impacted by the project.

Project Goal:
A project goal is a tangible statement of what the project should achieve.

Purpose:
Organizations start projects because they want to improve and grow. Describe the "deeper meaning" of WHY this project is initiated.
- What are we trying to accomplish with this project?
- Why is the project goal important?
- What are the long-term priorities of this project?

Impact:
Describe in as much detail as possible the impact this project will have so others can fully understand its significance.
- Who is this going to serve?
- For whom is achieving this goal important?
- Who else will be impacted?
- What is the most significant difference this project will make?
- What is the gain of achieving this goal?
- What is the pain of achieving this goal?
- What is the gain of doing nothing?
- What is the pain of doing nothing?

Outcome:
Imagine you have successfully completed the project; describe in detail what the results will look like:
- What does the final outcome look like?
- What will be different as a result of achieving this goal?

Success Indicators:
What needs to be in place for this project to be a success? How will you know the finished outcome is successful? What are the criteria to measure the project's success?

Know-how:
Describe what expertise and capabilities are required to successfully complete this project:
- What expertise and capabilities do we need?
- Who are the experts that we need to involve?
- What expertise and capabilities do we lack?
- Who can fill these expertise and capabilities gaps?

Influencers:
Identify project stakeholders. Be sure to include ALL the people listed under "IMPACT."
- Who is passionate about this project?
- Who else can help us move the project forward?
- Who has the power to pull the project back?

Figure 5. The Connect Card

The Connect Card is designed to provide a clear direction about who you should set up meetings with during the first 40 days of your assignment. You might not be able to fill out every aspect of the card at this stage and that's okay. Just filling in the card to the extent that you can will help you make progress and figure out who you need to look for. Once you start connecting with people on your Connect Card, they may be able to help you fill in the gaps and introduce you to the people who are important for your project.

Connecting with Your Team Members for the First Time

Of all the people on the Connect Card, the most important people you'll want to build trust with will be the people on your team. It's essential to connect with them on a human level from the very start. The best way to do this is to meet with each team member individually before you meet with them in a team setting.

The purpose of this first meeting is to get to know *who* the other person is. When it's time to meet your team member for the first time, set an intention for yourself to listen more than to speak so you can focus your attention entirely on the other person. When you enter these meetings with this mindset, people will absolutely feel it.

Full transparency is crucial in these meetings if you're going to gain the trust of your team. Some people may be considerably nervous or skeptical when meeting with you one-on-one for the first time. They may wonder whether you're approaching your assignment with hidden motives in mind, like assessing who can be fired or laid off to save on labor costs. They may fear that anything they share could be used against them in the future in some way. How can you make them feel at ease so their protective shell falls away?

First, be transparent about the process of the 100-day framework you intend to follow. Let them know that you intend to spend your first 40 days listening to everyone involved in the project so you can gain a clear understanding of the situation. Acknowledge that you don't have all the answers and want to learn as much as possible so you can lead the project and team effectively. Also explain what will happen next, including getting the team together and collaborating with them on a plan for achieving the goals you need to achieve. This will empower your team with the confidence that you're not just there to force your ideas on them or look for quick-fix solutions, but to implement a long-term plan that will incorporate the input and interests of everyone involved.

Next, explain your intention for scheduling this first meeting with them. Say something like, "Hey, I know we've just met. I'm really curious about you, your background, and where you come from. Then I'd like to understand what's going on for you business-wise, along with themes that are important to you. I want us to go through some questions together. I'll also share a bit about myself and some of the challenges you may be able to help me with. Would that be alright for you?"

At that point, make it clear that everything they share will always be used anonymously. People will share information with you to the extent that they feel they can trust you. By making it clear that *who* shares *what* will be kept confidential, you invite people to be themselves and communicate that you're primarily there to listen. You demonstrate that although you're there to solve problems, you don't necessarily have all the answers. You'll need the help of your team and whoever you're speaking with gets to be an integral part of that. Their feelings and opinions not only matter to you, but to how the project as a whole will unfold.

There should be three basic components to every first conversation during the connect phase:

1. Get to know their background and story.

Again, be intentional about being genuinely curious, asking questions, and staying in "listening mode." This meeting can be hugely informative regarding who the other person really is. Naturally, they're not likely to show all of themselves during your first meeting, but spend a bit of time hearing whatever they do want to share before moving on to talk about work. Practice active listening by keeping your attention on the present moment. Put your own thoughts, feelings, and judgments aside for the time being. Focus on what the other person is telling you without filtering their words through your own interpretations.

Here, you should operate in neutral gear. If you begin to feel triggered or sense judgment arising within you, you're already interpreting the information you're getting through your assumptions, beliefs, expectations, and native culture. Instead, stay curious and ask questions.

Helpful Questions to Cover During Your First Conversation

- Tell me about your background, education, and career so far. What's your journey in life been like up to this point?

- What's important to you in your life and your work?

- What are you most proud of, both personally and professionally?

- How's your family?

- What are your hobbies?

- What lights you up most?

- Where would you like to be in five to ten years?

Again, there's no need to pressure people to go deeper if you ask them a question they're not eager to answer. Just listen and make space for them to share in the areas where they feel comfortable. The questions above capture the three universal desires I mentioned previously: to be seen, to be respected, and to grow. If you're able to touch upon any or all of those desires at this stage of the conversation, you'll know you've made progress.

2. Understand the opportunities, challenges, or pain points they need help with.

Your next focus during your initial meetings should be to talk about how you can help the other person in your role as their leader. What challenges and pain points are they experiencing at work? How might you be able to alleviate that pain for them? As I mentioned in Part 1 of this book, you have to be willing to give before you can receive.

As they speak, pay attention to how they answer your questions. Do they talk mainly about opportunities or do they focus on challenges? Is their approach constructive or do they have a habit of complaining? This will tell you a lot about how the person is interpreting your organization's current strategy.

There are a number of other questions you can ask during this stage of the conversation to get a sense of how you can help the other person.

- What are some of the opportunities and challenges you've seen since you stepped into this role?

- What do you think are the strengths or weaknesses of our current strategy?

- If you were in my shoes, what would you change?

- How, in your opinion, could we use our resources more efficiently?

- What are three things you want to focus on in the next 100 days?

- How would you prioritize these three things?

3. Help them understand the opportunities, challenges, or pain points they are able to help you with.

Finally, once you've figured out how you can help the person you're talking with, you can move into the third stage of the conversation, which is to assess what they can help you with. This is the part where you share your personal story and background. Tell them about your vision, the project's mission, and what you're planning to do. You may ask some questions using your Connect Card. What knowledge and skills do they have? Who do they know that could fill some of the projects' capability gaps?

As you move through this part of your discussion, shift into a higher gear. You want to create enthusiasm about the kind of things you can do together. You want the people you talk with to get enthusiastic and think, "This person's capabilities could benefit us."

Dos and Don'ts of the Connect Phase

There are a few additional tips to follow if you're to build strong connections during the first forty days of your assignment.

- Meet with people in person whenever possible. Communication becomes much easier once you've spoken with someone face to face. If you absolutely have to meet with them online, be mindful about your approach. (I'll talk about how you can lead through the cloud in more depth in Chapter 12.)

- Maintain your relationships with headquarters or the senior management team that sent you on your assignment in the first place. You may believe that as long as you have everything under control locally and get the results you need, everything will be fine. This sets you up for the risk of miscommunication and subsequent misalignment on important matters. Rather than giving the people who sent you on your assignment the impression that no news is good news, keep them abreast of how things are unfolding on your end so you can collaborate when necessary.

- Be careful not to oversell yourself to your new team. There may be people with a desire to impress you during your first conversations, knowing you're the new boss and have a degree of control over their career. Don't fall into the trap of trying to impress *them* by talking about how good you are at what you do. Regardless of the intention behind this kind of behavior, there's a risk of portraying arrogance or giving the impression that you feel you know everything already. This would be counterproductive to building trust. The intention should be to be "interested" rather than "interesting."

SLOW DOWN NOW SO YOU CAN SPEED UP LATER

Leaders who have always defined success by financial results may find it difficult to build trust first because they're so results oriented. They want results as quickly as possible and consider building trust to be a time-consuming process. They lack patience and prioritize getting the numbers in. If this is you, try to reframe how you view building trust. Consider it an investment that will eventually get you the results you seek.

You are indeed in your role to get results. If there's one result you can deliver in your first three months, it's trust. View trust as a *deliverable* that's worth spending time and effort on right from the start. Once you've established trust with your team, getting financial results becomes so much easier.

One leader I spoke with, Ruth, Planning and Logistics Group Director for Bottling Investment Group, has experienced this in her role.

"When you start a new role, you have to make a decision. Do you want results now or do you want results that are lasting? I realized I wanted to build something that would be sustainable. When I'm building relationships, I really see them as results. I don't dismiss them. In my situation, I could have pushed for cost savings right away. That's a quick result. But the relationships are also results. From them, other business results will come, but they won't come immediately. I spent a lot of time at the beginning on building relationships. Now I feel comfortable enough to have discussions with people about cost savings and reduction, and they're comfortable with me. And I'm not imposing. I'm more like, 'Guys, we have to get such-and-such percentage down.' Then I ask, 'What have you tried so far?' Or I might show them an idea. 'Have you tried this or have you tried that?' And people don't see me as an outsider anymore. Making changes has become so much more effortless like that."

A former financial executive, Bret Packard, who is now leadership advisor and CEO of The Packard Network, shared with me a thought that captures the essence of the Connect phase well. He said,

> "The number one leadership trait is the ability to connect with others and have empathy. It's a very fundamental gap that has become huge and triggered all of these problems that are out there today with the Great Resignation and the War for Talent. As a leader, you have to support your people. How can I support you if I don't know how you feel? How can I possibly know what you feel if I don't ask you how you feel and what your personal needs are?"

I believe Bret was spot on. We can't act mindfully until we know, and we can't know until we ask.

In this chapter, we've focused on meeting with your team members, but there are likely to be people listed on your Connect Card who aren't part of your team. Building trust while connecting with those people is also necessary for the successful completion of your project. You can adapt the questions in this chapter for use in those conversations to create the level of depth you feel will be appropriate.

We've laid the foundation of trust in this phase of our framework, but trust is never built with others immediately. You'll have to meet with people regularly to create the solid bonds you desire. Over the course of future meetings, conversations, and encounters, trust will grow if you keep consciously setting an intention of genuine curiosity and focus on knowing the other person. Take advantage of each of these opportunities, whether you're communicating virtually or in person. With everything you say and do, strive to hit the touchpoints of the three universal human desires we covered earlier. Are you making people feel seen? Are you interacting with them respectfully? Are you tapping into their wisdom, knowledge, capabilities, and all their potential areas for growth?

The Connect phase is all about listening and conversing. Next, we're going to shift into the mode of consolidating and analyzing the valuable information you've collected thus far.

4

INSPIRE
Days 40 to 80

"It's logic that makes people think. It's emotion that makes people act."

—ANONYMOUS

ONE OF THE MOST COMMON QUESTIONS I HEAR BUSINESS LEAD-
ers grapple with is, "How do I inspire and motivate my team?"
This is no surprise considering Gallup has indicated just 21
percent of employees feel engaged and 19 percent are actively
disengaged at work. For the purposes of your new assignment,
now that you've built connections with your team, you'll need to
start focusing on two key requirements for inspiring them:

1. A clear vision

2. Buy-in

Without both vision and buy-in, making progress becomes difficult. You can have any number of brilliant ideas in mind for your strategy. If people aren't willing to follow them, however, you'll find yourself screaming into the void with no one there to listen. On the other hand, when you have buy-in without a clear vision, you end up taking people on a journey without a compass. You'll be popular but ineffective in the long run, which will ultimately cause your team to lose trust in your leadership. They'll no longer be willing to follow you because they'll lose faith that their efforts will end up making a difference. At that point, the spark of inspiration is extinguished.

This chapter will cover what you can do to develop a shared vision with your team and how to earn their buy-in in the process. To get there, I'll walk you through four steps that will enable you to make the most of the information you gathered in the Connect phase and distill it into a comprehensive strategy. They include consolidating the information you've gathered so far, working to comprehend that information, creating a new team identity based on a shared team purpose, and co-creating your team's plan for moving forward.

Your focus must be twofold during this stage. First, you must begin taking steps toward accomplishing your mission by figuring out how you'd like to roll out your strategy. At the same time, you have to get your team involved in forming that strategy with you. The key to this step is to create a new collective identity together. How can you form a bond with them based on what connects you all? What unites your team and what common ground do its members share? By finding the answers to these questions, the people you lead will tap into a sense of camaraderie over the things they all think and feel, which will, in turn, build excitement over the part they'll be playing within the group.

As you're working to inspire your team, it's crucial to keep in mind the three universal desires I shared in the last chapter. Everyone, regardless of where they were born and raised, wants to be seen, feel respected, and have the opportunity to grow. Their inspiration will stem not necessarily from who you are as a person, but from what you do, why you do it, and how all of that touches on what's important to *them*.

How can you touch on what's important to your team? In short, you'll want to incorporate their ideas, knowledge, experience, and opinions rather than pushing strategies from the top down. In this way, you form a *shared* vision that results in your team feeling seen and respected. The buy-in portion of inspiring them aligns with people's desire to grow. You want to offer your team something that makes them think, "I want to be part of this." They feel like they're part of a bigger mission and are proud to be contributing to it, as it will mean growth and progress for them as well.

Let's dive in, picking back up where we left off at the end of the last chapter. Where should you focus your attention after completing those initial meetings with your colleagues?

CONSOLIDATION

Once you've completed the Connect phase of your first 100 days, you'll have a wealth of information to work with moving forward. You may feel overwhelmed by all the data, ideas, opinions, and reports in front of you. How can you consolidate what you have now so you can make sense of the information in a way that will point you in the right direction?

First and foremost, remember your promise to keep the specifics of *who* said *what* confidential. You'll have to handle this in a way that allows everyone you're working with to remain anonymous.

Next, look back at the answers to the questions you asked during your initial conversations. What's the content of those answers and where do you notice similarities? What common themes did you hear come up frequently? By contrast, in what areas did people's answers differ? Additionally, pay attention to areas where your team members had little or nothing to say. Don't analyze or draw any conclusions about your observations just yet. Simply look at the info and make notes you can come back to later.

Once you've gathered your notes on what you heard, make two lists:

1.   What I Heard. (Here, make sure you separate *facts* from *interpretations*. The opinions and ideas shared with you by your team reflect *their* personal filters.)

2.   My Observations. (Write down what you picked up "between the lines." Remain mindful that these are *your* interpretations based on your personal filter.)

As you take notes, focus not only on differences of interpretation but similarities as well. It's easy to brush off matters that everyone sees the same way, but to do so is to miss a huge opportunity that will help you down the road. It's incredibly important to pay attention to which topics your people agree on because you'll need those components to build your team's new identity.

They'll need to know when others hold the same opinions they have. (Again, resist the urge to draw conclusions just yet. We'll get to that in a bit.)

A common example of an area where people may hold a variety of opinions is in regard to the budget allocated to your team. Some of them might, say, believe too much money is being spent on advertising. Others, however, might feel happy with how that money is being spent. Again, pause and consider the facts at hand. In this case, you have facts about how much is being spent. This data is neutral. Nothing about it is inherently good or bad. How people see things creates their interpretation. That thought process could be based on anything, from past experiences to cultural norms to personal beliefs. You don't have to judge or delve into that. Most of what was shared with you will center on subjective opinions, assumptions, and beliefs. What you need to notice is the fact that everyone brought up the advertising budget, which is likely because how it's being spent is affecting their work in some way.

As a final step of the consolidation process, prioritize the topics in front of you based on what you heard. If you've heard the same comments over and over again, it may be a big issue or something that needs your attention.

COMPREHENSION

After consolidating the information you collected, you'll want to ensure you've understood what it means to the best of your ability. Is what you *think* you heard accurate? Can you now use that information to reflect all of it back to your team in a way that's truly captured what's going on?

One way to handle this stage of the process is to set up quick check-ins with the people you connected with to verify what you talked about during your first conversation. By now, you've got a sense of the bigger picture of what's happening with your team. You've got more facts and opinions to work with. Get back in touch with the people who gave you that information and double-check its veracity by saying, "Here's what I heard during our conversation. Am I understanding correctly? Do you agree with my reflection of what you shared? Do you want to change or add something?"

You may find there are parts of your previous conversations that people will want to clarify or reword. They may wish to emphasize or reprioritize certain aspects of what they shared. There may be important things they forgot to mention. By opening the door for them to communicate further, you effectively lead by example, demonstrating that they don't need to get everything right the first time. You can question yourself and so can they. They're welcome to come to you when there's been miscommunication, errors, or inaccuracies. This shouldn't just apply to the members of your team, but your peers or other stakeholders as well. Checking back in with people to follow up, even if it's just online, serves as a powerful building block for the foundation of trust. It shows that you've listened, that you care, and that the opinions you heard matter to you.

Your First Group Meeting

The next step of the comprehension stage is to put the key points you've verified into a presentation you can anonymize and share with your team. Now is the time to bring together all the people who are going to be involved in the strategy driving your project.

Walk them through what you heard during your Connect phase and the observations you've made regarding that info. If you handle this well, no one will be able to tell who said what, but they'll be able to see what they shared and compare it to what others have shared. During this meeting people often find themselves saying, "I thought I was alone in thinking that!" It can be eye opening to get a sense of what's happening from a different perspective.

I recently spoke with Ebi Atawodi, Director of Product at Google and former Director of Product and Payments at Netflix, who found this step especially valuable. During her initial meetings with her team joining Netflix, she noticed that no one seemed to have the same definition of what the strategy was. None of them said this explicitly, but it was something she had observed. She was able to take that simple fact and reflect it back to her team during one of their first meetings. "Hey, there seem to be different interpretations of our strategy and how we plan to move forward." By drawing attention to this, she was able to get everyone on the same page through a targeted discussion.

The single most important thing you can do during your presentation is to emphasize to your team members what they have in common. There will almost certainly be differences at play, but focusing instead on what unites them in the beginning is key if you want to inspire. We're often wholly fixated on differences, but they're the connective tissue within your team that will pull people together. That's the breeding ground for co-creating the shared vision you're trying to achieve in order to implement a successful strategy. You can mention that there are points everyone may not agree on that you intend to tackle at a later date, but the time and place for focusing on those issues is not your first group meeting. This isn't about sticking your head in the sand.

Rather, it's about fostering a desire to collaborate. The last thing you'll ever want to do is sow discord among the members of your team.

You have a couple of main points to work with while creating your presentation. The first thing to draw attention to is the mission you've set out to accomplish in your assignment, which was given to you by your organization's board or executive team. Whatever that mission is dictates why you're there in the first place, and people will already be aware of what that is since you shared it during the Connect phase.

The second element to focus on is the common themes mentioned by your team. During the Connect phase, you asked them about the top three things they thought should be the focus of the next 100 days. During consolidation, you identified the points most people brought up over others. Those are issues you'll want to incorporate into the strategy you'll be building next as well.

WHO ARE WE? Creating a New Team Identity

At this point, many leaders make the mistake of bringing attention to the "what" too early.

What are we going to do and how are we going to do it? What would we need to do to achieve the results we need?

Rather than jumping right into forming strategies and tactics, focus on the question of "who." It's worth it to spend time solidifying a shared identity as a group. Think back to the Core Leadership Methodology illustration in Part 1. *Who* people are determines everything, including their actions, level of engagement, ways of interacting with others, and overall performance.

Who are we, both as individuals and as a team?

When considering who your team members are as individuals, take into consideration the degree to which they already know each other. The closeness of those relationships will vary across different organizations. Sometimes you'll be dealing with a team of people who have already been working together for twenty years. Other times, you'll step into teams of people who are completely new to each other. Either way, spend some time building team awareness around the unique people who comprise it. How can you all get to know each other a bit better?

Consider setting aside a bit of time to go through a few icebreaker activities that invite each person to talk about themselves. Even in long-term teams that have worked together for years, it's my experience that there are always a few surprises people didn't know about each other. Here are three activity ideas you can use to deepen the connections in the team.

The Lifeline Exercise

This is an exercise designed to encourage people to reflect on their lives and identities. They'll be given space to share moments or events that have had a profound impact on who they are today. Ask each person to write out a timeline and mark the key milestones of their life along its length. Once they have, ask them to pick one of the milestones that was truly life changing. It could be an event from their youth or something that happened in college. It might involve a move they made to a different city or country. Whatever they choose is valid as long as it's important to them. Go around the room and have each person talk about that experience, sharing how their life was changed by it and why. Set aside about ten minutes of presentation time per person. Ideally, have people prepare the lifeline drawing before the meeting, as it requires time and reflection to complete it.

Five Things in Common

For this activity, break your team up into smaller groups of three or four people and ask them to come up with five things they all have in common. Perhaps they've all traveled to Italy. Maybe they all like Indian food. Maybe they all have one sibling. Give them a few minutes to chat before asking them to share their answers with the rest of the team. The specific details they mention are secondary to the opportunity to find out more about each other.

A Point of Pride

For this exercise, go around the room and have each person share one thing they're really proud of personally or professionally. What's a significant accomplishment that's shaped who they are now? Why is it important to them? What was rewarding about achieving that goal? As they share, people will likely begin to recognize similarities in each other or gain a better understanding of what lights each other up.

In some environments, you're likely to experience some initial backlash when you introduce these activities. People might wonder what the point is or feel as if they're wasting their time. They might feel as if they already know each other well, or hesitate to talk about personal stuff at work. In cases like these, stay in high gear and reiterate the goal of each exercise. From experience, leaders tell me that when their team members start talking about themselves and their past, everyone ends up learning valuable new information that provides ground for unity in the long run.

After exploring the "who" at the individual level, you can move on to exploring who your team is as a group. This involves having one or more conversations focused on creating a sense of identity around who they'll need to be as a team in order to be successful. To have them create a Team Purpose, you can use these questions to start the conversation.

- Who do we want to be as a team to achieve our goals?

- What is it about this team that makes us unique so we can deliver what our stakeholders need?

- What can we do uniquely that no other part of the organization can do?

- What can we do uniquely together that we cannot achieve when working in silos or parallel to one another?

- What do we want as a team that we can only do through collaboration?

- What does a winning team look like?

- What are the benefits for all of us, based on our collaboration and interdependence?

- What strengths would we need as a team to be able to respond rapidly and positively?

- What do we want to be known for? What's the reputation we want to build?

As I mentioned before, there will almost certainly be differences among your team, some of which they'll already be cognizant of. They'll have different backgrounds, experiences, opinions, and perspectives. Some of these differences can actually be a core strength of the team, as diversity of thought can bring rise to innovative ideas. When possible, look at differences among your team members as an advantage.

One leader I worked with, who was part of a tech company in the healthcare industry, shared with me the team identity she and her people came up with as a result of this discussion. Together, they zeroed in on five points they could all agree on.

1. We are a team that helps the organization grow business in the healthcare sector locally. We speak the local language.

2. As a team, we are a community where people can feel a sense of belonging.

3. We represent an aspirational place that people want to be part of.

4. We see and understand the needs and achieve sustainable, customized solutions to serve all stakeholders.

5. Everything we do in tech has a bigger impact.

Ebi, who I mentioned earlier, worked as a leader at Uber before and felt that identifying a team's uniqueness gives it a superpower. As an example, she shared with me an experience with a team based in India that was responsible for the emerging markets. They had to figure out how to deliver Uber's services to buyers who only had feature phones. When they started their project, the Uber app was only available to markets with smartphones and high-speed internet. The team gathered insights across all Uber markets and built a new version of Uber they could use in all emerging markets. This became their superpower. Uber teams worldwide began contacting them for insights on emerging markets. If they could build their tool for India, they could do the same anywhere. This became the group's identity. "If you work with us, we can give you insights on how to solve problems related to emerging markets."

Another idea for solidifying your new team's identity is to establish team values. Have them do the value exercise you did in Chapter 3. What values are important for the whole team? What are your team's nonnegotiables?

By finding out what aligns your team, you'll help unite them in ways that go beyond culture, politics, religion, and other historically divisive interests. When you invite them to contribute to the process of forming this collective identity, you give them clear concepts they can take pride in as a group. They'll be inspired to come to work thinking, "This is who we are and I'm excited to be involved."

HOW DO WE WIN? Co-creating the Plan

After your team's identity has been defined, it's time to move on to forming your strategy. The main question here is, "How do we win?" How can everyone work together to achieve what you and the team are there to do?

Though that question starts with "how," you're not going to be able to answer it without the buy-in of your team. If you begin this discussion by dictating *how* you want the plan to be carried out, you risk losing them, as they're likely to feel like you're telling them how to do their jobs. It's worth keeping in mind that your team has likely already tried out a number of strategies to address the problems they're facing. The "how" has to be a co-creation. On your end as the leader, you'll do best at this point by focusing on the "what." What are you trying to achieve as a group? What is your shared vision for success?

As I mentioned before, you have two big pieces of work to organize: your assignment and the topics that came up in the Connect phase. These will have to be broken down into smaller goals, so initiate your discussion about the "what" by prioritizing them according to their themes and associated projects. With your team, analyze what you can do to cover the largest part of your collective workload. Together, take some time to prioritize that list.

Now divide your team in a way that makes sense so they can focus on forming a strategy around their specific contribution. Leaders are likely to divide their teams according to knowledge and expertise as per the Connect Card. Each of your subgroups will be responsible for tackling one specific theme or topic on behalf of the rest of the team.

Martin started a new role as Managing Director for Vander-Lande in India. He had a management team of nine people total and divided them into three subgroups of three. The first subgroup was responsible for the team's growth plan. How could they achieve the vision of growth for their division? The second subgroup was responsible for people and competence. They were tasked with figuring out the team's strategy for attracting and retaining the best talent to support their division's growth. The third team was responsible for forming a team strategy for speeding up innovation. How could they accelerate innovation within their division? By delegating each of these tasks, Martin was able to get his team on board with the plan they created together. There were discussions and differences in opinion, as there often will be, but overall, people felt the urge to buy into what was proposed because their own ideas were incorporated and carried out.

As the leader, your role in this space is to provide clarity on the direction your team should be heading, as well as corporate strategy insights your team may not be aware of. If they come up with ideas that don't match what your organization wants or needs, that's where you'll need to step in and steer their trajectory in another direction. You can also offer them frameworks and methods for developing business and team strategies.

A final piece of advice for this stage is to assign your subgroups smaller tasks early on to establish quick wins. Pick a few of the relatively easier projects your team wants to accomplish within your first 100 days, delegate them, and keep deadlines short. If your team has the opportunity to show early success, you'll instill a broader sense of trust and inspire those who haven't yet bought in to get on board. Help them develop faith that what you decide on together can work.

HOW DO WE ENGAGE? Forming Team Agreements

Anytime something goes wrong within a team, it's because the people involved had different expectations in mind for how things should go. This shouldn't come as a surprise, as your team members will all have different backgrounds and experiences. They may have seemingly incompatible styles of working when you all come together as a unit. Effective team fluidity doesn't happen naturally; details around team functionality must be discussed with intention to avoid misalignment.

Rather than getting caught in the mess of clashing expectations, it's better to make agreements about how things will be handled within your team. What can you all commit to? What best practices can you all agree on while working together? What type of leadership behavior would you like to see as a team? How will your group identity and values translate in the way you collaborate?

For example, if your team identity has been built around "safety," what does that mean for how you'll all work in your team, and with your peers and customers? How will an identity around "safety" influence your decision-making?

As another example, if your team identity is built around "customer centricity" and putting customers at the core of all decision-making, what will that look like? What are the indicators that you're actually making that happen? An example of an indicator could be: *we prioritize customer needs over our own needs* or, *we want to look at situations through the eyes of the customer.*

The next step is to create team agreements and policies of *how* you want to work together. This will help everyone avoid misunderstandings and communication issues down the road. It will also boost everyone's feelings of ownership and accountability in relation to your project. People are far more likely to stick to agreements they've made than to feel a sense of ownership over terms that have been dictated to them. Your team will care more about living up to their side of bargains they had a hand in creating.

Here are some examples of team agreements that will help everyone remain in high, or at least neutral, gear together.

How to Handle Meetings

Here are a few examples of agreements around team meetings:

- "We set clear meeting goals so we're conscious about how we'll spend our time together." (This may involve things like brainstorming, active discussions, and decision-making.)

- "We all show up. If we can't attend for some reason, we notify our team leader and send a representative in our place who has been briefed in advance and can actively contribute."

- "We all have a set number of hours on our calendars for meetings across time zones when everyone is available."

Communication Protocols

Another agreement among your team members might center on how to handle communication. Who should be notified and how when someone can't attend a meeting or other event? When should the team use tools like email, WhatsApp, Zoom, or phone calls?

In the past, my teams and I have arranged protocols around these questions. For longer messages pertaining to nonurgent matters, email felt appropriate. For more urgent matters, WhatsApp and phone calls made more sense. You might also make agreements around communication involving decision structures and spending budgets, as well as agreements that keep things running smoothly when team members work remotely (see Chapter 12). All of these measures can go a long way to mitigate miscommunication over time.

Decision-Making

Create clear agreements about the decision-making process. Team decision-making is great, but it should be clear from the beginning what will happen if the team can't reach a consensus. Obviously, you and the team can't know upfront *what* the decision will be, but it should be clear *how* a decision will be reached in these cases. Will it be you, the leader, who makes the final decision? Will there be a vote? If so, will the option that gains a majority of votes win? Will the decision made after the vote be binding or simply advised?

High-Gear Influence

At this point, you've divided your team into subgroups so they can work on forming the strategies that will make up your overall plan. You're likely organizing regular meetings to establish and roll that plan out, measure progress, and dig into the nitty gritty details of the work.

As your project unfolds, there's much you can do to help keep your team performing in high gear. At their best, they'll be more motivated, inspired, and solution focused. Many leaders underestimate the influence they have over the state of mind of their team members. The energy you bring into a room, whether that room is real or virtual, can set the tone for entire meetings. Your attitude has the power to either boost everyone's spirits or drain them of energy. Let's explore some ways to keep your team feeling inspired.

Focus on Process, Not Outcome

Most leaders feel the need to put importance on very specific outcomes. Much of our energy goes into achieving results that are measured against metrics-based goals like sales numbers, budgets, turnover, and other fixed targets. These goals are meant to indicate whether you've been successful or not. When you exceed a sales budget, you know you're on track. When you don't, it feels like you or the team have failed.

The outcome-focused approach involves a lot of judgment. If you let it drive your thought process, your team will likely feel like they're not good enough when they don't achieve the desired results. This can lead to a loss of individual and collective self-esteem. The most frustrating element of these situations is that we can't, in reality, always control the outcome of business ventures. Your team's mission will be influenced by market volatility, the competition, the economy, and many other factors. Focusing solely on outcome can lead you to believe you and your team failed when that's not actually the case.

When I work with clients, I take a different approach to setting goals and measuring results. I view goals and targets as part of a larger improvement process that consists of a combination of planning, taking action, evaluating results, and making adjustments when necessary. This forms a loop you must always be looking at. When you take this approach, results aren't the only factors taken into account. Every step toward improvement in the process is valuable. More importantly, those four steps make each step of your assignments more manageable and encourage you to focus on what's within your control.

Let's look at the Olympics as an example of the approach I'm mentioning here. Many athletes who train for the Games have the ultimate goal of winning a gold medal. There's a four-year run-up to the Olympics, however. How can anyone stay inspired for four years? To keep up their motivation, athletes set smaller goals to work on throughout their training process. If they're a swimmer, they might work on getting off the starting block faster, making their turns smoother, or decreasing their lap time by a tenth of a second. These are small steps they have full control over and achieving them provides the motivation they need to keep going. During the Games themselves, athletes have little control over the outcome. They can't control the conditions of the pool, the fitness level of their competition, or what time they'll be competing. So, they focus on getting stronger, fitter, faster, and optimizing their process.

Taking a process-oriented approach isn't about letting go of your goals and results, but instead using them as an assessment mechanism. Only look at results as a source of feedback to evaluate how well your process is working. This strategy will give you and your team a mindset focused on mastery and growth. When things don't work out, don't take it as a sign *you* have failed. There are simply *process steps* that worked out differently than expected. Those can be changed, adjusted, or optimized to give you different results.

What to Do When Inspiring Others Gets Hard

As mentioned before, to successfully guide teams through a change, two things are needed: a clear vision and buy-in. While both are equally important, more often I see leaders struggling to get the full buy-in of the entire team. They have to deal with one or more individuals who don't seem to want to get on board and are openly or quietly resisting the change.

The key in these situations is to understand the true reason for resistance. What goes on in the minds of people who resist change? Many times, team members will agree with the overall vision, but oppose the "social" aspects of the change—what it means to them in relation to others.

In short: there is *fear*. Resistance is a *reaction* that comes from a place of fear.

- People feel *anxious*, self-conscious, and vulnerable.

- People worry about what they will *lose* as a result of the change.

- People believe there are not enough *resources*.

- People feel they are not *ready* to change.

- People are *tired* of changes.

As a result, people would rather *keep* things as they are.

Even if the above thoughts and feelings are present, that doesn't mean people will vocalize them. Resistance can be active and open; more often it is passive, where people show signs of resistance by procrastinating, making excuses about why "things are not done," saying yes but not following through, etc.

Aim to "coach" rather than "manage" people through change. When we *fear* something, we make assumptions and create scenarios in our minds about what *can* happen as a result of the change. It's those assumptions and scenarios that cause our fear. The only way to respond to fear is with empathy.

A Process to Help People Accept Change

1. Sit down with them and listen to their concerns. Acknowledge and validate the other person's feelings. "It's normal to feel [the way you feel] given what's going on."

2. Ask questions about what they *believe* will happen. You may need to do some exploring to find out what's important to them and what aspect of the change they feel particularly challenged by.

3. As you learn more about their fears, discuss how you can help make plans that will support them during the change.

4. Remain nonjudgmental.

Questions to Ask

- What aspects of the change do you think you have no control over?

- What aspects of the change do you have control over?

- What do you believe will happen after the change is made?

- What makes you feel challenged when it comes to the change?

- What do you feel might be benefits for you when it comes to the change?

- What's the worst that could happen?

- How likely is that to happen?

- What are some of the things you can do to prevent that from happening?

- What plan can you have in place in case that does happen?

- What would you need to feel more comfortable going through the change?

- How can I support you in this?

Be Mindful of the Language You Use

In every interaction, meeting, email, and conversation we have, we can choose whether or not to operate from high gear. We have to be conscious of these opportunities to use our language in ways that create optimal outcomes. Always consider how you might be able to add value to the situations happening around you. How can you use your conversations to take your team dynamics to a higher level? Keep in mind that everything is energy. The way you talk, the words you use, and the tone of your voice can completely shift the atmosphere at any point.

Here are some examples of low-gear language and corresponding high-gear alternatives.

LOW GEAR	HIGH GEAR
"We have a problem."	"I need us to find a creative solution."
"This situation is catastrophic."	"What's the opportunity here?"
"Ted is a difficult person."	"Ted's a character."
"She's very aggressive."	"She's assertive."
"That's an unrealistic assessment."	"That's an optimistic assessment."

As you can see and likely feel for yourself, speaking from the high-gear standpoint creates a totally different mood. Sometimes the way you speak and the energy behind your words can be enough to inspire someone and turn their entire day around.

UNDERSTANDING POWER

Dr. Martin Luther King Jr. defined power as "the ability to achieve purpose and effect change." The concept of power often comes with a negative connotation, but Dr. King Jr.'s definition demonstrates how it can be used to inspire others rather than oppress them.

True power is not something we own and hoard for ourselves, as that type of power is based in fear. Fear, as we all know, is never a solid foundation from which to widen our sphere of influence or work effectively with others. Fear-based power leads to micromanaging tendencies, as leaders who succumb to it strive to attain full control. They dictate rather than coach people in order to support their thinking and behavior. They see themselves as separate from others and view the world from a place of judgment. They think in limitations and conditions, and easily blame other people and external circumstances for what they perceive as problems. They're driven by winning and enjoy seeing their competition lose. Their ego-driven need to be on top and advance their personal interests is shortsighted in the long run. When we help others succeed, we succeed right alongside them. People who wield fear-based power rarely, if ever, get the opportunity to enjoy that experience.

True power is something we *give* to others. Competent leaders share that power while collaborating in order to see people grow and benefit from it. They share information, lead with empathy, take ownership, are open to feedback, and operate from high gear. How they lead brings out other people's talents and gifts. They're driven by the desire to create rather than compete. They foster inspiration rather than insisting their way be the only way of doing things. People are automatically inspired by and follow leaders who work in this way, as their approach evokes a feeling of growth for all.

In the next chapter, we'll explore how you can use your leadership power to help the people you work with grow. By the end of your assignment, they'll have to be able to thrive on their own, without your oversight.

5

GROW

From Day 80 Onward

"Every talent we cultivate brings to the mind the desire to cultivate another talent; we are subject to the urge of life, seeking expression, which ever drives us on to know more, to do more, and to be more."

—WALLACE D. WATTLES

ALL ORGANIZATIONS SEEK TO GROW OVER TIME, BUT THEIR ability to do so hinges on the career growth of those they employ. A 2011 global study performed by the *Harvard Business Review* found that only 15 percent of companies in North America and Asia believed they had enough qualified successors for key positions. In Europe, fewer than 30 percent of organizations felt confident about the quality and amount of talent in their pipelines. In the context of emerging markets where companies were focused on developing their growth strategies, the supply of experienced managers was most limited, and this shortage was predicted to continue for at least another two decades. These predictions were correct. If the post-pandemic War for Talent taught us anything, it's that this problem has gotten worse and will almost certainly continue to do so in the near future. When we fail to facilitate the growth of our people, we end up with too few high potentials to fill key strategic management roles, which jeopardizes a company's growth or expansion plans.

Let's revisit the three universal human desires: all people want to be seen, feel respected, and have the opportunity to grow. When it comes to building and maintaining high-performing teams, the big question boils down to how we cannot only hang onto high-potential candidates and talented employees, but also how to recruit them. Some global assignments will require you to lead an existing team, but in the case of emerging markets, you'll often be sent abroad and tasked with building a team from scratch. The people you hire will then need to grow their professional skills and knowledge throughout your mission, but also want their careers to continue after you're gone. If the people you lead feel they are stagnating, your long-term progress will be dead in the water.

In this chapter, I'm going to cover the final phase of the Connect, Inspire, Grow framework, which centers on the essential concept of (you guessed it) growth. This topic applies to all of us because, at our core, we all want to grow. This desire is encoded in our DNA, present in everyone. Everything we humans do is rooted in a wish for more. We want more knowledge, skills, money, luxury, joy, fun, love, or happiness. This all stems from our eternal yearning for a fuller expression of life.

There's nothing wrong with our desire for more. It's entirely natural for us to have hopes and aspirations because they motivate us to take action. They drive us to progress and expand as people. We have a deep, instinctual understanding that when we don't grow, we get stuck. Anything in nature that doesn't grow dies. I notice this phenomenon during conversations with people I work with all the time. When people feel stuck in some way, they're unhappy or experience stress. They want to develop and express themselves in areas that matter to them rather than feeling like they're being held back.

People are always more attracted to leaders who provide them with a sense of growth. If you're operating from high gear, sharing your power, and focusing on driving continuous improvement, people will want to work with you regardless of whether they're team members, clients, peers, or stakeholders. This will happen because you operate on the premise of "We can only win when we all win," meaning that a win for you is a win for everyone.

When you bring this attitude to the table, everyone will be able to sense it. Colleagues will want to team up with you. Clients will want to do business with you. If you want your mission to succeed, pay attention to how you empower others. Talented people thrive in an environment that "breathes" growth and expansion. You want a team that's going to win and continue to grow right alongside you. Let's start by talking about how you can attract the right talent to your team.

TALENT RECRUITMENT

Over the last few decades, the traditional approach to recruitment has centered on seeking out people with hard skills. The most qualified, technically skilled candidates were the most sought after in the job market. In the last chapter, we talked about focusing on process rather than outcome and how this leads to continuous improvement for the entire team. If we're to create a team culture that lends itself to this type of dynamic, we need to start looking at a different set of capabilities while hiring people. Ideally, you want to be looking for lifelong learners who are curious, creative, innovative thinkers, and adept collaborators. As you interview candidates, ask them about their experiences in these areas, making sure to mention these elements are part of the role they're applying for. Long-term team growth is better served via these characteristics as opposed to a high I.Q. or perfect scores in school.

I had an interesting conversation with one of my clients the other day. He's an Australian business executive currently leading an immensely talented team for one of the biggest brands in the world. His team recently earned the highest score in the region in an employee engagement survey. Many of his high performers end up moving on as they're promoted to other roles. He jokingly complains, "I train all these superstars and they end up leaving me in the end!" But he takes genuine pride in the opportunities they're given and is always excited to see their leadership skills get recognized and rewarded. He is slightly concerned, though, about how he can sustain the high-performing culture of his team as he recruits new talent to replace his rising superstars. Our conversation centered around this dilemma.

"What kind of people do I want to bring in next?" he asked me. "Should I look for people whose values align with what's made our team successful so far, or should I hire field experts who understand our sector and look great on paper?"

Our conversation boiled down to the key question, "Is team culture more important than outcome?"

I asked him, "To what extent do you believe there should be an equal reward for input versus outcome?" In my view, team input consists of all the collaborative efforts our talent brings to the table. Outcome, on the other hand, consists of the results we achieve.

My client had to think about his answer to my question. Finally, he said, "Deep down, I believe that culture is driving the right outcome. I've always believed that. I'm now comfortable establishing and maintaining that culture for current and future success. I want to retain that growth mindset and focus more on the process than the outcome. I'm not that fussed about how *others* are determining success. We have our own measures of success, and they have brought us the results and engagement we have today."

I admired the powerful insight he demonstrated with that statement. He was able to solve his own dilemma by listening to his intuition and going back to what he believed to be true about what would be best for *his* team instead of looking to conventional standards for success.

"It's a bit selfish as well," he said, smiling, "to hire talent based on characteristics rather than formal qualifications because there are huge benefits in doing that. I can coach and train people to make sure they have the knowledge, but I don't need to coach them on culture. Everybody can learn the hard skills, but forming a team culture itself is far more difficult. If we click on that level during interviews, they're in. The rest will sort itself out."

When it comes to talent recruitment, we also have to begin looking at the available talent pool differently. The idea that there's a shortage of qualified candidates implies there aren't many people out there for us to choose from. If there's one big lesson the pandemic taught us, it's that you don't necessarily have to seek out talent that lives within a fifty mile radius of the office anymore. Remote working has allowed organizations to tap into a much wider area to fill their talent gaps. American companies, for instance, can now recruit people in Europe or the Middle East. People's willingness to work remotely has grown, meaning the talent pool has actually gotten bigger, not smaller. As you seek out new members for your team, consider whether expanding your recruitment radius might build a stronger team for your mission in the long run.

TALENT RETENTION

The topic of team growth also relates directly to talent retention. Another consequence of the COVID pandemic was that it forced us all to pause our lives and rethink our priorities. People took the time to ask themselves, "What's most important to me in my life? How do I want to spend my time throughout the eight to ten hours of my workday?"

When it comes to our work, there are many more intrinsic motivators at play than there used to be. In the past, a good salary, a plush office, and a nice company car might have been enough. These days, what drives people has changed and become more personalized. Many people want a better work-life balance, but the "why" behind that desire is different for each individual.

In Chapter 3, I talked about sussing out that "why" during your initial meetings with each of your team members during the Connect phase. At this stage, you'll want to revisit the question of what growth and development mean for them on a personal level. The key to modern talent retention is to personalize this rather than attempting a one-size-fits-all approach. How can you meet people's growth ambitions when growth for them means, for example, more free time to take care of their kids or elderly parents? How about those for whom growth means taking four months off to climb Mount Everest, or getting experience working in different areas of your organization, or accelerating their career to become a senior leader within the next five years? If you believe the talent is there, how are you going to facilitate that personalized type of growth?

According to a 2022 McKinsey global survey, employees who feel like they don't have access to avenues for learning, growth, and development are 41 percent more likely to quit. While leaders may assume it's up to HR to create talent development programs to avoid this from happening, that will not be enough.

The same report stated 34 percent of people surveyed mentioned the reason they quit their jobs was because of uncaring and uninspiring leaders. This is a warning signal for team leaders who underestimate the value of connecting with their people and taking ownership of their influence. Talent retention efforts start with you. By following the framework in this part of this book, you'll be far less likely to lose talent you want to keep.

COMPENSATION

As I mentioned before, I often hear leaders complain when employees leave because they can make a dollar or two more elsewhere. The feelings of those leaders are valid, but they may misunderstand that often it's about more than money alone.

For many people, money isn't just about economic value, but emotional value as well. To them, money represents recognition and respect. Whether or not that idea is accurate is not the point. The point is that people who perceive money this way and feel they're not compensated well still leave due to not feeling valued.

Traditionally, organizations have rewarded employees based on the position they hold and the amount of experience they have. Some also receive bonuses when they go above and beyond in performance. But if you want to develop a culture of continuous improvement first and foremost, driven by people who show up in a way that's aligned with your team values, you need to be willing to have that reflected in how you compensate people.

I've coached quite a few incredibly talented people, all of whom worked in top-ranking global consultancy firms, who sought coaching because they felt stuck in their careers. They had climbed the corporate ladder and made it to the higher ranks of the organization, only to find out once they arrived at the top that they felt unfulfilled and discontent. They had hoped to find more interesting projects to work on so they could grow and bring meaning and purpose to their work. Instead, all they found were greedy partners who didn't want to share high-profile work because they wanted to keep a bigger piece of the financial pie, including the bonus.

How do these things happen? Essentially, these people were being compensated for their *output* alone—not for adhering to company values like equality, fairness, talent growth, and team collaboration. Companies working on the level of strategic relationships, which we covered in Chapter 3, create a golden cage that drives talented people with valuable skills away from their organization.

If you want people to focus on their input—things like collaboration, teamwork, creativity, and taking ownership—you will want to start being innovative about how you measure success based on input and behavior. Start rewarding people for that.

HOW TO HELP YOUR PEOPLE GROW

At this stage of your first 100 days, you've connected with your team, built your strategy, and are rolling out that strategy bit by bit. How can you monitor that everything is going according to plan on a day-to-day basis while helping your team continuously improve? To ensure this happens, I like to have what I call "grow-based meetings," which are intended to facilitate team development while providing guidance and support. I divide them into two categories: team meetings and individual meetings. What you do and discuss during these interactions will depend on what you're aiming to accomplish in that moment.

Three Types of Grow-Based Team Meetings

Check-In Meetings (or Standups)

Check-in meetings are weekly meetings that allow team members to discuss challenges or roadblocks that pop up throughout the project, come up with collaborative solutions, and share what they are going to be working on for the week. You can steer these meetings to ensure they're focused on helping everyone grow. Here are six actions you might consider incorporating as you prepare for them each week:

1. Send updates on the content of previous meetings to team members ahead of time.

2. Set a clear agenda.

3. Celebrate progress made.

4. Discuss ongoing projects and challenges.

5. Allow each team member to share what they are working on, along with the opportunity to ask for help if needed.

6. Document individual and collective action.

The importance of holding regular check-in meetings cannot be overstated. Think of them in terms of how you take care of your health on an ongoing basis. You check your blood pressure and monitor other ways your body is evolving. Similarly, you want to keep your finger on the pulse of your mission. Is your team really making progress? Are they doing what they're supposed to be doing? Are they sustaining an efficient state of well-being? These meetings focus on your project's building blocks and ignoring or being inconsistent with them can result in serious consequences down the road.

Umesh Madhyan from Bottling Investment Group told me he's known for *never* missing check-in meetings. Nobody on his team misses them either. He holds them every Monday at 2:30 p.m. without fail, fifty-two weeks a year. If anyone is on leave, they delegate someone to take their place. No function goes without being reviewed. This is one of their core team agreements that has always served them well. If you're sloppy about check-ins, you're sure to miss important details about what's happening.

Brainstorming Meetings

Brainstorming meetings are short get-togethers with the team. The goal here is to come up with as many ideas as possible to tackle a particular challenge, solve a problem, or accelerate progress on a specific goal. The key to effectiveness is to focus on the ideas themselves rather than outcome. Here are five rules you can follow to make your brainstorm meetings a success.

1. Every idea matters. No judgment or criticism are allowed. In fact, it's ideal to encourage your team to think of the most outrageous solutions they can, as those ideas may contain elements you'll be able to use. Bad ideas don't exist.

2. Build on other people's ideas. If someone proposes an idea, rather than responding with "but," use "and" instead.

3. Avoid focusing on the "how," as it can lead to dismissive tendencies. You don't want to shut anyone down by responding to an idea with, "Yeah, but *how* would we do that? That's not going to work." Focus on the idea itself.

4. Represent ideas visually whenever possible. Use whiteboards, Post-its, or virtual tools to write down what's being proposed. This triggers the brain to think of more ideas rather than spending energy on keeping them in mind.

5. Set a time limit of thirty minutes. Studies have shown half an hour is the ideal window for generating creative output. On top of that, setting a time limit forces the brain to think more quickly.

By following these rules, you'll be able to involve your entire team in forming solutions. They'll feel heard and valued knowing their opinions matter.

Money Matters Meetings

These are team meetings relating to money, whether you're dealing with project financing, new investments, budget monitoring, or other financial concerns. Here are some steps you can take to make the most of your time.

- Send out the numbers you'll be discussing prior to the meeting. This will prevent your team members from having to sort through data while you're all together. Your meetings themselves should only revolve around discussion and decision-making.

- Remain focused on the main issues at hand. Don't get lost in the details, as this will only hold everyone up. By the time the meeting is over, you should always have accomplished what you set out to do in your agenda.

- If you find yourself feeling surprised about any aspect of your financial reports, take it as a warning sign that something is off about your process. Your budget may be wrong. Your team may not be building what you all agreed upon. There may be a link missing between your co-created plan, budget, and the decisions you've made thus far. The point is not to blame anyone when you pick up on red flags, but to reassess your team's process. Reflect this attitude in the language you use so you can keep your team in high gear. If you're ahead of the budget, great! Acknowledge and celebrate that positive feedback. If you're behind the budget, don't treat that information as "bad" or "disappointing" news. It's just feedback based on a number that shows you your process needs adjusting. Talk about what can be done to improve how things are being handled among your team members so you can change that result.

Two Types of Individual Grow-Based Meetings

Feed-Forward Meetings

We often talk about feed*back* meetings, but I'd like to propose what are called "feed-*forward* meetings" instead. This concept was developed by executive coach Marshall Goldsmith, who observed that focusing on strategies related to the future ended up being more effective for helping teams grow than focusing on past events.

In traditional feedback meetings, employees receive information about how they're presently performing or have performed. Feed-forward meetings, by contrast, center on a wide variety of future opportunities. For example, let's say one of your team members gave a presentation and it didn't go as expected. Instead of providing them with details about how their presentation skills were ineffective, you can give them guidance, recommendations, and encouragement on how they can get their message across more effectively in the future. This approach is more likely to keep them in high gear. Rather than focusing on what they might perceive as judgment or failure, they'll feel supported in imagining how they can grow in ways that lead to better outcomes. The past is the past. It cannot be changed. Therefore, it's not worth it to linger there.

Development Meetings

These are regular meetings, usually held monthly, where you can talk with your current team members about what keeps them satisfied, happy, and engaged in their job. You want to form a clear picture of what each person values about working with your organization and support them in terms of the direction they want to head next. Many companies hold exit interviews to gain feedback on why employees have decided to move on. Considerable time and energy are put into this, but the fact is that by that time, most people won't see the worth in being honest about their reasons for leaving. It's more effective to invest that time and energy in your current team. Here's a list of questions you can ask during development meetings.

- What is it that's making you want to stay here with us?

- What aspects of your work excite you/fulfill you/are you content with?

- What's working? What's not working? What's missing?

- What are you looking forward to at work now and in the future?

- What are some things that you still want to learn?

- What are things that would help you grow?

- Where do you see yourself in the next one to three years?

- What needs to happen for you to get there?

DEVELOPMENT PLANS

Use the answers to the questions above to create a development plan that's customized to suit the other person's growth-related needs and desires. How can you support them with their health and wellness goals, future role aspirations, succession planning, work-life balance, and flexible work arrangements?

If people want support in their current role or in preparation for their next role, there are three broad ways to help. The first is growing their knowledge, which can include business knowledge, industry or sector knowledge, product knowledge, or technical knowledge. The second is growing their skills, such as leadership skills, communication skills, problem-solving skills, or job-related technical skills. The third is developing their behavior. This can include taking ownership, collaboration, building trust-based relationships, or proactiveness. For each development goal they share with you, define the required level of knowledge, skills, or behavior they'll need to reach it.

It's also important to keep in mind that people don't all learn in the same way. Some people learn better through experience. Some learn better visually. Some learn best through exposure to new people, networks, or work methods. Others want more formal education or to attend workshops. For leadership skills and behavior, you might propose that they work with a professional coach who can tap into their individual potential or a mentor who can guide them in their specific role. There are all kinds of ways you might help someone grow in these areas. The crucial element here is to brainstorm co-creative solutions and come up with a plan that will work for both of you.

For example, say a member of your team has a goal of moving from a regional to a global role within the next eighteen months. Have a conversation with them about what they'll need to be successful. What knowledge or skills are they missing? Do they understand the related parts of the business well enough? Perhaps they would benefit from spending six months working in another division, if that's feasible, to gain experience there. Perhaps you'd like to see them lead others more effectively before that point and choose to hire an executive coach to help them grow their self-awareness. See what you can come up with while forming their development plan.

GROWING YOUR TEAM THROUGH LEADING BY EXAMPLE

One of the most powerful ways to grow your team is to model the kind of leadership behavior you'd like to encourage. We all learn by mimicking the people who teach us the skills we need to succeed. How can you lead by example?

Ask versus Tell

Do you manage your team or coach them? The difference here is in how you approach communication.

Managing a team consists of *telling* them what to do. Here, you're focusing on specific tasks.

- *"You should..."*

- *"You need to..."*

- *"You had better..."*

- *"Do (this/that)."*

- *"Don't do (this/that)."*

Remember, your employees want to be seen, feel respected, and grow. Telling them what to do will likely achieve the opposite.

Coaching a team is accomplished by *asking*. Here, you're focusing on empowering people. Asking people questions will give them the experience of being involved in finding solutions. They'll feel you're interested in their opinions and providing them with opportunities to learn.

Have you noticed yourself telling rather than asking? If so, how can you shift your leadership style from one of management to coaching?

First and foremost, anytime you hear yourself telling, stop in that moment and realize what you're doing. You don't want whoever you're speaking with to feel belittled or mistrusted, nor do you want to risk making them feel defensive. In that moment, try to reframe what you're saying as a question. How can you accomplish what you're trying to accomplish by asking instead? Here are some examples of questions you might ask.

- What's another way you could go about completing this task?

- What could you do to help in this situation?

- What ideas can you come up with that would lead to a different outcome?

- What are some ways you might improve this further?

- How do you think we could accomplish that?

- What would you need to change to achieve that?

- What's working, what's not working, and what's missing?

- How does this work for you?

- What's the benefit of doing it this way?

- What's the downside of doing it this way?

- What's your plan?

- How did you arrive at this outcome?

- What assumptions might you be making?

- How else could you look at this situation?

- What would you need to know to make that decision?

These kinds of questions can open your team up to all kinds of choices and possibilities. They also demonstrate that you find them resourceful, value their contributions, and want to help them grow into the greatest version of themselves. You're not approaching them as if you've got all the answers. That's okay. No one does. Instead, you're getting curious about their perspective and inviting them to try seeing things from a different angle. You're also inviting them to share the reasoning underlying the direction they wish to take because, who knows, it could end up being better than what you've got in mind. You might end up compromising with them to arrive at a solution that incorporates both of your perspectives. This will help you continue to build trust with your team and model respectful, constructive behavior as you move through the Grow phase.

Stay Connected

By now, you may be anywhere from three to six months into your role. It's very common at this point for leaders to get so involved in their day-to-day tasks with their team that they forget about connecting with their relevant stakeholders.

Take a look back at your Connect Card from Chapter 3. Is there anyone listed there who you haven't been in contact with during this phase of your assignment? If so, it's best to reach out to reconnect with them. Some stakeholders may change roles. Some who weren't important at the start of the process become more important as your assignment progresses. Ensure you keep your conversations with all those people alive. Over time, people's lives can change. So can their opinions. They may have changed their mind about certain things or want to know more about what's happening. If you're connecting regularly with the influencers around your assignment, you'll continually build trust and be more likely to keep their support. They'll be genuinely interested in how you and your team are doing and how your mission is taking shape.

Additionally, consider setting aside two or three hours in your schedule each week to have conversations with people in your organization you don't know well. You'll have to be seen as someone with an interest in advancing everyone, from team members to clients to other colleagues who may be outside the group of stakeholders you identified for your mission. The objective of these conversations is to connect, learn, offer help, bring value to others, and build your network.

Martin does this on a regular basis. He's based in Holland and is responsible for leading over 800 people in India. He travels there once a month and stays for one to two weeks. Before he leaves for these trips, he has his personal assistant plan two meetings a week with random employees from the Indian organization.

I recently interviewed him about this strategy.

> "It's so much fun. The employees are super excited to talk with me for that half hour we're together. They know this is something I do regularly, so when their turn pops up, they're super excited to finally talk with me. I keep the atmosphere casual and informal and invite them to ask me questions about anything they want. There are always a handful of things I want to know from them in return. What keeps them busy? What are their main challenges? What are they proud of? What's happening for them that week? I'm now more than two years into my role and have learned so much through doing this. I plan to continue doing so because listening to the voices of people on the front lines creates enthusiasm, provides insight, and gives me the chance to connect with about 100 people per year. That's very valuable and important for me."

You can adopt a similar strategy by setting aside a few hours in your schedule for unscheduled conversations. Walk the floor of your organization and ask people how they're doing. If you do this regularly, people won't shy away when they see you or treat you like "the big boss" in the ivory tower. They'll see you as a colleague who knows and cares about them. Someone who's on the same level rather than above them. This makes you accessible for anyone to share ideas and opinions with, without having to go through formal hierarchical structures.

Foster Curiosity

Harvard University published research measuring the level of curiosity of new employees just starting their jobs to their level of curiosity eight months later. By the six-month mark, employee curiosity had dropped by 20 percent. The survey also showed that 92 percent of people valued curiosity, as it inspires innovative ideas within teams and organizations more broadly. Curiosity is also a catalyst for job satisfaction, motivation, and high performance. Other benefits of curiosity include fewer decision-making errors, less group conflict, more open communication, better team performance, and more diverse networks. Only 24 percent of respondents said they felt curious at work, while 70 percent said they faced barriers to asking questions.

You can keep people curious by continually asking them *why* and *what-if* questions: "What is one piece of work that you are curious about today? What if you changed the routine of one thing you usually take for granted?" In turn, invite *them* to ask you those questions and challenge the status quo. Make it clear that you're open to receiving feedback.

Celebrate

Celebration is a huge aspect of both personal and professional growth. In our day-to-day lives, we often forget to spend time celebrating individual or team accomplishments. We're busy, focused on progress, and want to move right onto working toward our next milestone. This is understandable, but try to make celebrating a habit within your team.

Celebrating even the smallest win stimulates a dopamine release in the brain. That feel-good chemical reinforces the growth experience and strengthens our sense of connection to the people we work with. Change and growth are promoted through positive emotions. Find ways to celebrate and recognize people's input. Don't just acknowledge the results they create, but also the efforts they're making to get them. You can also celebrate project kickoffs to relay excitement about the journey you and your team are embarking on together. You don't have to overdo this or make it a big deal. Keep celebrations authentic and meaningful. Simply press pause and take a moment to honor the value people are contributing. Being able to look back over your shoulder and express appreciation for the amazing goals your team has accomplished is a habit that creates a celebratory mindset in your people.

Don't Let Ego Get in the Way

When you're in the midst of meetings and conversations, don't allow your own ego or anyone else's to take over. Everyone's opinions are equally valid, therefore it makes no sense to get defensive while working together to solve problems. It's just a sign that you or other people have shifted into reverse gear. Stay curious. Encourage others to share their opinions. Stay mindful of the difference between the facts and feelings at hand. All of your discussions should aim for progress and growth.

When conflicts pop up in regard to personal or professional differences, resist the urge to take it personally and shift back into high gear. Ask questions that will move everyone forward.

- "How are we going to grow from this?"

- "How can we move forward and make progress?"

- "How can we make sure this doesn't happen again?"

- "What can we do differently here?"

With these growth-oriented questions, you can move on from arguments about who did what or what went wrong.

Failure Doesn't Exist

There's no such thing as truly failing. There's only learning. A failure-focused mindset creates judgment against yourself and possibly others as well. When something you try doesn't work, that's just feedback that signals your process needs adjusting. Don't dwell in disappointment, shame, or other low-gear emotions.

Think about how sports teams approach losing games. If a football or basketball team performs poorly, they don't have the luxury of beating themselves or one another up over it. (At least, not for long.) They've got another game the next day to prepare for. We can take a page from their book to gear ourselves toward doing better in our next "game." We can stay in high gear, embrace challenges, and become comfortable in discomfort.

How can you keep that feeling fresh during the Grow phase? I suggest looking for lessons in other people's successes rather than being competitive toward whoever you may be "losing" to. What did the "winners" do to achieve their goal? Notice whatever it is and learn.

Set Yourself Up for Future Growth

You don't want to remain in your role longer than necessary, as doing so can prevent you from advancing in your own career. If you don't want to end up getting stuck, your number one priority should be to build your team's confidence in their ability to run the business independently of you.

You may wonder, "How will I know my team is ready to take the reins?" It's a fair question. The framework I've covered here is only meant to span your first 100 days, but they won't be ready to function on their own by that point. Truthfully, you'll *never* know if your team is truly ready because the business world as a whole is volatile and unpredictable. You'll never get to a point where your team is guaranteed to handle every deal, investment, project, process, or venture smoothly after you step away.

The only thing you can do while helping them grow is to put complete trust in them so they'll feel like they *can* do it. Too often, we unintentionally do the opposite. We destroy trust. We want to keep control. We fear letting go of our power. You don't want to end up in that position as it will stifle everyone's potential, including your own.

Here are nine questions you can ask yourself to get a sense of whether you're preparing your team to operate independently of you.

1. How do you show your people that you have confidence in their skills and abilities? How often do you do this?

2. How do you show your team that you care about them?

3. How do you give your people the opportunity to make decisions? How often do you do that?

4. How do you encourage your people to take risks?

5. How do you build an environment where they can learn from their mistakes?

6. How do you celebrate the team's successes exuberantly?

7. How well do the things you do and say express your trust in the team?

8. How openly do you share information with your team?

9. How much do you invest in their personal and professional development?

Your team's confidence regarding their ability to thrive without you doesn't hinge on their past achievements. It's based on the belief they'll be able to handle any situation that arises. We can never know or control exactly what will happen in the future, but we can operate from the feeling that no matter what pops up, we'll figure it out. Once that feeling is in place, *that's* when you can move on.

Your team's success is your success. Focus on facilitating them and providing guidance so they can do the best job they can. By keeping *their* growth a priority, you're growing their leadership skills. The goal here is to have one or more people lined up to take over from you.

How to Grow Yourself

Here's how you can grow yourself throughout your assignment:

- **Get mentors, coaches, and advisors.** Don't feel you have to go at this alone. Intellectual loneliness is common. You can avoid it by always surrounding yourself with people who challenge your thinking and give you direct and honest feedback.

- **Keep mentally fit.** Your mind is your most powerful tool. Multitasking is a myth, so train your mind by focusing on one thing at a time. Don't wait too long while making decisions. Indecisiveness takes up a lot of mental space and can keep you stuck. Making a decision, even if it is the wrong decision, keeps you moving forward. Decisions are hardly ever permanent. More often there is an opportunity to change things, including your mind, if things turn out differently than you hoped.

- **Keep physically fit.** A healthy body and mind will have real, significant impacts on your leadership style. Food, alcohol, and coffee consumption, exercise, and sleep or lack thereof all play a major role in your performance.

- **Balance is a necessity.** You need to fill your cup first to be able to give to others. Don't forget about what energizes you and brings you joy. Remember your purpose— *why* you wanted this.

The Connect, Inspire, Grow framework we've covered in this part of this book provides a basis for you to work from as you make your way through challenges during the first 100 days of your assignment. That's not to ignore the fact that people in your position often confront particular challenges depending on what their mission is, where they're working from, and where they're coming from. More often than not, these processes don't end up unfolding as smoothly as we'd like them to. As we move through the next part of this book, I'm going to discuss the seven biggest challenges I've seen in my work and proven ways to overcome them.

PART 3

SEVEN MAJOR CHALLENGES OF LEADING GLOBAL TEAMS

6

LOST IN TRANSLATION

When Culture Becomes
a Source of Friction

"The world in which you were born is just one model of reality. Other cultures are not failed attempts at being you; they are unique manifestations of the human spirit."

—WADE DAVIS

IN MY RESEARCH I INTERVIEWED ARJAN DE BOER, A DUTCH senior banking executive who was promoted to a global position in Hong Kong in 2010. He had already been working in Asia as the regional head of a private international bank when he was offered a new role as Head of Private Banking for Northern Asia. He had more than five years of experience living in Singapore and had traveled to Hong Kong on a monthly basis. His wife, who he'd been married to for years, had Asian roots. He was well acquainted with Asian culture, or so he thought, and accepted the job with excitement.

After he moved to Hong Kong and stepped into his role, Arjan soon discovered he'd greatly underestimated the challenges associated with his new position and location. "It was a huge culture shock," he told me. "Hong Kong is profoundly different from Singapore. At the time, Singapore was an international city with an Asian flavor. Hong Kong, on the other hand, was deeply Chinese to the core."

At thirty-seven years old, Arjan was also faced with a merger with another bank and considerable employee turnover. More than half his team left within six months. The people he was in charge of were less loyal and committed than he'd been expecting.

"Before I went, I thought I knew what I was stepping into, but the reality was quite different. This was like being in the arena and I got very close to calling it quits. I just felt really burned out."

In spite of his wealth of experience, cultural differences threw Arjan for such a loop that he began doubting his own capabilities. Arjan eventually managed to get things under control, but his story is far from unique for executives entering international roles in countries that are new to them. In this chapter, I'm going to discuss steps you can take to avoid getting swept up in a similar spiral abroad.

WHAT'S THE CHALLENGE?

The culture gap is one of the most commonly mentioned reasons for what many refer to as "expat failure." In the past, business leaders on missions abroad tended only to have to deal with one foreign culture. In today's business world, it's more often the case that leaders will have to lead multicultural teams with members from all over the world, or lead multiple global teams in different countries doing a majority of their work online. This new norm presents an extra challenge, particularly in the area of communication. Building trust, as I discussed in Chapter 3, must happen first and foremost. So the basic question becomes, how can you build trust across cultures?

There are two parts to this process. The first involves you, the leader, interacting and building trust with people from other cultures. The second involves the members of your team building trust with each other so they can work together productively, which you are also responsible for facilitating. This means that multiple lines of trust need to be built simultaneously, which can make things somewhat complex.

People like Geert Hofstede and Erin Meyer have done a considerable amount of research on cultural differences and their implications for leaders. Both have written books on the subject that I highly recommend reading in preparation for your new role. Don't limit your preparations to surface-level workshops on cultural etiquette or articles on topics like how to give and receive business cards. You'll need to delve far deeper if you're to be truly prepared.

In addition to any reading or research you do, talk to people who have worked similar roles to the position you'll be entering, particularly if they've worked in the same country or office you'll be going to. They'll be able to pass on more comprehensive knowledge so you'll get a feel for the more important aspects of different cultures—the way people interact and communicate, their cultural values, as well as how they deal with elements of leadership like hierarchy, negotiation, and decision-making. What's their concept of time and punctuality? How do people deal with rules and agreements? All of these considerations will be waiting for you when you arrive.

As someone who has worked extensively in China, I was initially taken aback by the difference in importance given to contracts. In much of the Western world, a contract is a legally binding document. Once the parties involved sign it, they're expected to adhere to its agreements relating to the work that will be done, how each party will be paid, and when. Contracts are referenced when doubts arise about the details and scope of a project. In China, however, a contract is merely a piece of paper that represents the beginning of a professional relationship. The scope of the work can change massively over time and if you don't adopt a relatively flexible approach, people there will see you as rigid and unadaptable. When that happens, projects flounder.

Knowing about these different cultural aspects is one thing, but when you work with multicultural teams, you want to *discuss* these topics and make team agreements about them to avoid confusion. (See Chapter 4 for specific recommendations on team agreements to make.) Culture will have to continue to be a topic of conversation to grow awareness for *all* stakeholders involved in your assignment.

BEHIND THE CHALLENGE: EXCESSIVE FOCUS ON DIFFERENCES

I've spoken to many leaders who, like Arjan, did everything they could to prepare for their assignment abroad and still ended up running into a wall of confusion after arrival. They couldn't seem to move things forward with their new team and couldn't pinpoint the underlying cause of the problem. Many people in this situation blame what they perceive to be irreconcilable cultural differences, but to do so sidesteps the root of these issues.

When we're abroad, it's natural to focus on differences rather than the things we share with local people. The books, research, and cultural awareness trainings I mentioned earlier—all well researched, extremely valuable resources—tend to focus on those differences and how they impact business dealings in the host country. This tendency isn't unique to international environments. The evening news is saturated with stories of conflicts among people of different backgrounds, ethnicities, or socioeconomic groups. When we start fixating on differences, eventually that's all we see. This comes with a risk of stereotyping the people we work with. I hear too many leaders sigh and complain in frustration about cultural characteristics in general terms, applying their views to every person born in the country.

"Chinese people only care about what the boss wants."

"Americans are too opinionated, always butting in to say what they think."

"The Germans are so rigid."

"The Japanese are overly polite and cautious."

The desire to generalize is natural, but we have to remain realistic and in high gear while doing so. There are certainly tendencies in behavior and communication that hold true across different regions, but culture only comprises *one* aspect of a person's being. It's part of who we are, but not *all* we are, and stereotypes can blind us to that fact.

When we're willing to go a level deeper into the self, we can appreciate that we are, in essence, all part of the same wider human culture. There's far more that unites than divides us. This should be your focus as you work with your team. If you remain fixated on the things you don't have in common, you'll have a lot more work to do while building a relationship of trust with them.

As I explained in previous chapters, the more we focus on connecting with people and *who* they really are and what drives them, the more easily we can support them in what they need, making them more willing to contribute. We can collaborate, engage, negotiate, and have healthy disagreements as a team, all while being clear about our common goals, sharing fun experiences, and generating results. This hinges on the sense of relatedness we leaders foster at the beginning of our assignment.

I've seen some leaders struggle, lose their patience, and take on an authoritarian leadership style as a default response to things not working out as they wished. They assume if they don't, they won't be taken seriously. Creating that emotional distance, especially while you're trying to build trust with your team, won't lend itself to success in the long run, even if you believe you're doing so in the name of professionalism. On the contrary, emanating an air of superiority is likely to cause fear of failure in others and result in reactiveness instead of proactiveness. You'll get less creativity, less engagement, less transparency, and less information sharing.

Connecting at the human level, which I described back in Chapter 3, reduces judgment and increases understanding. By creating an environment where this is the status quo, people can begin to relax, let their guard down, and show more of themselves and what they are capable of. They'll also be more excited about talking and working with you.

HOW TO OVERCOME THE CHALLENGE

Helen Spencer-Oatey, Professor Emeritus of Intercultural Communication in the Department of Applied Linguistics at the University of Warwick, wrote, "Culture is a fuzzy set of basic assumptions and values, orientations to life, beliefs, policies, procedures, and behavioral conventions that are shared by a group of people, and that influence (but do not determine) each member's behavior and their interpretations of the "meaning" of other people's behavior."

In other words, cultural differences can *by definition* never be the only reason for expat "failure" or unsuccessful projects. Human behavior and communication can be messy in all contexts, and throwing culture into the mix can certainly be a complicating factor. But your role as a leader working across cultures is to help your team notice the potential *influence* of culture in their often complex and changing environments. To do that effectively, you'll need to draw out the true perspectives of the people you work with. Don't assume they'll think or feel a certain way based on what you believe to be true about their cultural background. That will only make you likely to miss out on key information.

We've all been living in a globalized world for quite some time now. Some of your team members may have spent years living on a completely different continent. If you approach them with what you know about their native culture or country in mind, you won't be giving credit to the individual experiences that formed their views and opinions. In a multicultural environment, there are bound to be multiple "truths" and perspectives. Listening carefully to people's opinions and ideas and looking for places of agreement rather than disagreement will be key to bridging these gaps.

Leading across cultures means that we have to notice and stay in conversation about that cultural piece of us that *may* be at play in a situation. Here are a handful of points that may help you during that process.

Know Yourself

In addition to the tools and practices mentioned in Chapter 1, we can also develop self-awareness around how our own culture influences our leadership skills. For example, I'm of Dutch origin and our organizations are often characterized by a lack of hierarchy. As employees, we approach our bosses and senior managers easily, calling them by their first names. We're also known for our directness. We don't beat around the bush or hesitate to openly challenge our superiors' points of view. I've come to learn, having spent almost fifteen years living and working abroad, that our open and honest approach can be considered blunt to the point of rudeness by people from other cultures. I'm more aware of this now. I still ask for what I need, but depending on where I am, I may use a different tone or choose different words to express my thoughts, be conscious of the social setting, or approach people one-on-one. While doing business abroad, I ask my local colleagues what they think about an issue before sharing my interpretation of the facts or challenging someone on theirs. I make an effort not only to understand others, but also to help them understand me.

Throughout your assignment, you'll inevitably learn more about the unique intricacies of your own culture than you ever did while living back home. You'll be confronted with the ways in which *you* might seem "strange" or "different" to them. You'll get insight into particular behaviors that have the potential to raise eyebrows. Always be aware that disagreements that pop up may have nothing to do with your local colleagues and everything to do with *you*. You'll never be able to anticipate exactly how you'll come across to others. The best you can do is try to be open, humble, and curious about what's actually going on.

Servaas Chorus, a Head of Corporate Banking, was born in the Netherlands and is currently responsible for teams in Europe, the Middle East, and Africa. He talked to me about challenges he was experiencing related to the culture gap. After nearly twenty-five years working with the same bank on assignments in London, Warsaw, Amsterdam, New York, Shanghai, and Hong Kong, he was offered a job back in Western Europe where he'd been raised.

"When I started working in New York," he said, "I realized why Europeans are so effective here. My experience was that Americans, in general, take orders pretty well. Western European people like myself are very critical and outspoken. Even though the American people are known to be more extroverted, they sometimes had more fear of speaking up than I did. They would hold back about expressing certain opinions while I spoke my mind. This approach worked for me there. People found it refreshing. Then I moved to Singapore and Hong Kong and spent over seven years in Asia. But now that I'm back in Europe after so many years, I'm having to deal with people who are critical in the same way I was critical in the past. It took me a lot more time to get buy-in than I wanted it to take. I really had to ask myself, 'How do I connect with people to get their trust?'"

For Servaas, being confronted with his own culture after working overseas for so long was incredibly difficult. The people he ultimately had the most trouble working with ended up being those who were similar to his younger self. The experience allowed him to realize how the time he spent abroad had influenced his leadership style in ways that made him more effective.

"Once you get back to your own country," he said, "it seems that things have suddenly changed. But the reality for people who have moved around the world is that the experience changes *you*."

Honor Differences

When I say that we as leaders should focus on human similarities rather than cultural differences, I don't mean to imply we should *ignore* those differences. During the Inspire phase of your first 100 days, which you can review in Chapter 4, you can enhance your meetings around building team identity by acknowledging and honoring the ways in which your people are unique. Bring your own culture into those conversations as well, as that will make it easier for your team to understand where you're coming from.

People are often very proud of where they come from. Again, culture doesn't comprise the whole of their being, but it plays a part that they may be excited to share. Look for the beauty in their stories. Indulge in whatever they may want to show you. When they invite you to join them in a local tradition or invite you to their home, it's often a sign that they want you to be a part of what they're proud of. This is a terrific opportunity to build the next layer of trust with them.

Martin had something to say about this during our interview.

> "I'm open to understanding why people may think differently and why things may be done differently. What helped me in China was being open to becoming part of their pride. I often had to attend dinners and drink baijiu (a local spirit with a high alcohol percentage). Even if you don't like the taste, you do this out of positivity and openness toward the local culture. You don't judge it but engage in it. Now, I try to do the same in India. There are days when you don't really feel like having another Indian food night. But if your Indian colleagues invite you to their favorite restaurant because it serves the best local Indian food, which they love and are proud of, you join them. It offers you another opportunity to get to know people in a different way and ask questions about their culture."

I know for a fact that Martin walks the talk in this sense. I saw him a couple months ago in a photo on social media covered in colorful paint at the Holi Indian festival. It's easy to see how his willingness to throw himself into any adventure that arises earns him respect. When he worked in China, people told him, "You're becoming more Chinese every day!" Now in India, the people he works with express similar sentiments.

Ask For and Get Feedback

While you're abroad, you're bound to encounter many moments when you're lost in translation, noticing behavior and customs that, in your view, make no sense at all. Your brain will automatically try to make sense of these situations by filling itself in with interpretations or assumptions based on what you know. This is your brain's shortcut for analyzing situations that are new. When you find yourself doing this, ask those around you what they believe is happening.

"What do you make of this? I see...which makes me think...but what do you see? What am I missing here?"

Getting feedback on how you lead from people you trust is essential. It's difficult to see our own filters and how they color our views. Having a few people from different cultural backgrounds who are willing to be honest with you can help you get a more objective sense of how situations are unfolding. In some cultures, you can have conversations with your team members directly. In others, people may feel uncomfortable opening up to their supervisor, as they're mainly used to top-down communication. See if you can ask peers or get external support from a coach or trusted advisor with no agenda other than to help you.

Create a New Team Identity

As we discussed in Chapter 4, creating a new team identity can go a long way in bridging cultural gaps. Again, it's not just on you to build trust with your team members. They must also build trust among themselves. You've got to spend time creating space for them to get to know each other and what makes them unique as a team. Focus on bolstering interdependence among them so they can effectively pursue their common purpose. What unites them? What makes them stand out as a group? How can they be successful as a group? What are they trying to achieve together and how can their unique experiences feed into that? Building that team culture will allow them to form that trust you seek. They'll be able to develop a sense of pride, collectiveness, and belonging, and take ownership of what they've created together based on the ways they're united. Everyone in the organization must know what they stand for.

In my interview with Ebi Atawodi, who's originally from Nigeria, we talked about her time working for Uber in Amsterdam. She led a team of people from India, France, the Netherlands, Sweden, and Nigeria who had to work with partner teams in the US. A major cultural hurdle they worked through together was how to deliver feedback effectively.

> "We all had different perceptions of how to deliver feedback. The Nigerians, for instance, like those of us from the Netherlands, can be far more direct in their communication style than, say, the Americans on the team. There was potential for some people to take offense in these situations, while others thought nothing of it."

As a leader, you have to understand these cultural nuances. Part of shaping the culture of the team is having them work toward compromise, not demanding that anyone put up with discomfort, but by forming team agreements around feedback that are unique to them.

Anticipate the necessity of creating a new and unique team culture that's designed to serve everyone involved. Having those conversations shows that you're considerate and respect the diversity of cultures within the team. It will not only get everyone onto the same page, but give people who've helped shape the new culture a reason to feel excited and proud of their involvement. There's no right or wrong answer that will work for everyone. Come up with team values that suit *them*.

Understand That Trust Is Built in Different Ways

Building trust is done in different ways in different countries. Something you'll want to find out early is how you can present yourself as a credible person who's competent in their role. The *Harvard Business Review* published a piece of research involving executives from the US, Asia, Latin America, and the Middle East. The focus of the study was how well they all understood the importance of results versus character as elements of trust building, mentioning that cultures generally emphasize one or the other. In the US, trust in the workplace is generally based on results. If you say you're going to deliver by a certain deadline and you do, people will trust you'll likely deliver according to deadlines in the future. In the Middle East, however, trust is built on character. If someone is referred to you by a family member or trusted colleague, you'll likely trust them automatically. Many companies in the Middle East are family owned and run.

In Japan, people build trust based on character as well, which one client of mine soon discovered while working there. Johan, although born in Europe, had spent many years in the US working for The Coca-Cola Company and held a relatively senior role despite being only thirty-four years old at the time. Unfortunately for him, age is a major factor in trustworthiness in Japan. This made things quite difficult for him in the beginning, because most of the employees directly reporting to him were in their fifties. People were cautious.

"Even when they acknowledged what I was saying in conversation," he told me, "there was no guarantee that what I needed them to do would get done."

Luckily for my client, he had a phenomenal manager who had been in a similar situation previously. This manager advised him to take on an older executive assistant, a sixty-five-year-old Japanese man who had spent his whole career working for Coca-Cola. He was fluent in English, energetic, and wanted to get things done. My client brought him to every meeting as his right-hand man and had him lead discussions in a context that appealed to the local staff. Over time, as they got to know him and understand the reasoning behind his decisions, they began to trust him and everything ran more smoothly. He was finally taken seriously by his team based on his own merits thanks to the older gentleman who had assisted him. Without that man, Johan's assignment in Japan would probably have progressed more slowly. Creating a new strategy around how he could build trust with people and meeting them where they were at were key to moving things forward.

Connect at the Human Level

The more you connect with your team and get to know specific things about them, their stories, their concerns, and their aspirations, the deeper your relationship with them will go. You'll increasingly be able to see they may not actually be all that different from you after all. Cultural differences will matter less and less, even with those you initially perceive as furthest from you in values. You may have initially felt triggered by them, assuming you had nothing in common with each other. If you keep reaching out, they may in fact turn into the most interesting people you've ever known. These human-level relationships (as discussed in Chapter 3) can turn out to be essential in difficult times and situations. You'll want those substantive connections at your back as you navigate challenging environments.

Relish the Adventure

You wouldn't be in this role if you didn't have a "lust" for adventure, fun, and excitement. Patience and understanding are essential here as well, so stay curious while remaining as far as you can from judgment and biases. Don't take anything anyone says to you personally. Nothing is *ever* personal, as we know, as everything people think and feel has been run through the filter of their interpretation. People say and do things for their own reasons, which have nothing to do with you.

Being lost in translation can feel frustrating and confusing. You may feel inclined to cruise in a lower gear. Don't stay there. Switch back into high gear and keep going. If you see everything as a problem and a struggle, that's what your world will look like. But if you keep being curious and open-minded, you'll see the opportunity for fun in the midst of the mess as well. Embrace and relish the adventure as it unfolds around you.

7

THE OCEAN OF THE UNKNOWN

When You're Not the Subject Matter Expert

"To know what you know and what you do not know, that is true knowledge."

—CONFUCIUS

HUMANS TEND TO FEAR THE UNKNOWN MORE THAN NEARLY anything else. When you're unsure of how things are likely to turn out, the future can be incredibly daunting. This is particularly true in professional situations where you're stepping into a new environment and have to lead a project or team when you're not an expert in the subject matter at hand. What skills should you apply here? How can you add value while not having all the technical knowledge?

Most companies choose to send their senior executives abroad for three reasons. One is to fill a position that requires a particular type of expertise that needs to be transferred, like technical or managerial knowledge. The second is managerial development, allowing the leader to gain international experience so they can take on future roles within the company. The third is organizational development, which aligns both the leader and local managers with the corporate culture and creates a network that provides links between subsidiaries and headquarters.

Not all job promotions are based on expertise in a particular field. You may have been awarded your new role as an opportunity to grow your career by expanding your knowledge and gaining experience working in an area of the organization that's currently unfamiliar to you. I've seen this happen, for example, to leaders working in finance who are sent to spend a couple of years in purchasing, or people who go from product development into operations to gain more understanding of what's happening at the front end of the organization. Sometimes you'll be asked to take assignments that entail these lateral moves. Other times, you may make the choice to continue your career in a different industry or business discipline. Either way, such transitions can end up causing us to feel additional pressure to perform.

In this chapter, we'll discuss how you can dive into the ocean of the unknown and navigate its waters with boldness and grace.

WHAT'S THE CHALLENGE?

Stepping into a completely new field is both exciting and scary. It's a bit like being lost on your first day at a new school where everyone knows each other, but you don't seem to know anything. All eyes will be on you. If you've worked with your organization for a while by that point, you may have built credibility elsewhere in other departments. In those cases, your reputation may precede you. However, chances are that if you're in this situation, you'll be expected to start managing people who have all the knowledge and expertise you lack. They'll expect you to enter the situation with an effective vision and strategy that will allow you to start steering the ship in the right direction from day one. You may not have any clue what problems they face or how things are typically handled in that field. When you find your team looking to you expectantly for guidance you don't necessarily have access to yet, what will you do?

In the best-case scenario, you'll have prepared well for this situation by speaking to colleagues with experience in your new line of work. This will, at the very least, give you a basic sense of what's going on. In the worst-case scenario, however, you'll have been given nothing but a briefing on your mission and a set of targets to hit by your senior management. Then, off you go into uncharted waters.

BEHIND THE CHALLENGE: THE RISK OF DIVING IN TOO QUICKLY

If you're faced with these situations, you might start by filling your calendar with meetings. You want to fill the uncomfortable gap of "not knowing" with "information." There's a strong fear you won't be taken seriously since you're unable to make informed decisions, caught off guard by jargon or language you don't understand. In short, you're afraid to fail, and this fear causes you to focus on two things: your own insecurities, and how to gather as much information as possible. You ask questions, take notes, gather data, and then walk away from meetings armed with information and opinions. The team doesn't get to know who you are at this stage, and you feel unable to properly connect and inspire because you have no clear vision yet.

I've seen three things happen when leaders focus mainly on collecting information in these initial meetings. The first outcome is that you may end up taking more than giving, as you'll feel that's all you're in a position to offer at that point. You'll give a short introduction, possibly mention your past achievements, ask a series of questions, take notes, and soon the meeting will be over. The people on your team will have expectations about meeting their new boss for the first time. They'll be curious and perhaps even a bit anxious to meet you. Upon noticing your frazzled focus on collecting information, they'll quickly realize you're not paying attention to who they are at all. They might still get the impression you're a nice person, but more likely than not, they'll be disappointed because you didn't give them anything. *You* may walk away wiser, but they will not, effectively establishing a one-way, transactional relationship rather than a collaborative exchange rooted in connection.

The second possible outcome of diving into these situations before connecting and establishing some trust with your new team is that people will tell you only what's safe for them to share. They're highly unlikely to give you honest insight on deeply rooted challenges percolating beneath the surface. They won't yet know you, won't trust you, and may fear what could happen to the information they give you. It could end up landing in the wrong place or coming back to bite them at their next performance review. The more you push, the more reluctant they'll become, afraid of the risk of you winning at their expense. Not a good place to be.

The third possible outcome is that you'll walk away from your initial meetings with only half of the story of what's actually happening. This will be partly due to people's reluctance to open up to you immediately, but also due to the fact that you'll be hearing only from the most extroverted members of the group. There will be team members who will want to make a good impression. Some will exaggerate or underplay certain situations, or possibly even brag about their contributions. Those who are introverted or less vocal won't speak up unless specifically asked. Therefore, the entirety of what you hear will represent only a fraction of the big picture. Being that you've only just met those people and won't be familiar enough with whatever team dynamics are going on to distinguish truth from fiction, you'll question how valuable the information you've gathered actually is.

HOW TO OVERCOME THE CHALLENGE

There are a few key points to follow in order to conquer the ocean of the unknown.

Build Trust First

Though it's tempting to dive into the deep end right off the bat and attempt to devour as much of the information you're missing as possible, focusing on building trust first will serve you better. People will tell you only what you need to know once they trust you. You can deal with this by taking the approach I covered in

Chapter 3, which focuses on connecting during the first 40 days of a global assignment.

Create a Circle of Knowledge

Use your time and energy to strategically create a circle of knowledge around you. Try to get a sense as quickly as possible of who knows what. You don't need to try to catch up to the people around you who have worked in the industry for years by learning everything they already know. That will only land you in an excessive number of meetings that will make you feel completely overwhelmed.

Find out who you should rely on for certain types of skills and expertise. I suggest using the Connect Card I shared in Chapter 3, which will help you sort out exactly what you're trying to achieve in your initial conversations, what kind of know-how you have on the team, and where the gaps are. This will save both you and your team a fair amount of time. You'll be able to structure your meetings in ways that target the specific people you need to speak to while leaving out those you don't.

Don't Focus on Yourself

I've seen many leaders who tend to be too self-centered encounter more challenges when it comes to building trust with others. There are two reasons behind this type of behavior. The first is the fear of failure I already mentioned. You may be thinking, "My God, how will I come across? What will everyone think of me?" These types of thoughts can be paralyzing and prevent you from hearing what others are saying. You may be rightfully concerned about reaching your own targets and getting results quickly, but fixating on this too deeply will distract and overwhelm you. You'll be focused on proving yourself and focused on winning. When *you* winning becomes more important than the team winning, this will surely backfire at some point down the road. Realize that you can win only when they win.

It's possible to operate from a place of egotism without being aware of it, but this will always have a detrimental effect on the team. I'll tell you a story of what happened early on in my career to give you the employee perspective.

I worked in sales on a team that was assigned a new director from outside the organization who was new to the industry. During our initial meetings with him, which typically ran two to three hours longer than scheduled, he came off as extremely busy. He asked us questions about our processes, wanted to know about our customers, and asked us to prepare numerous additional reports on top of all the standard sales reports that were already available. It felt like we had to provide loads of information and always clear our schedules when he was in town, and he was focused entirely on his own agenda.

We never quite knew where he was or what he was up to. When we needed to get a hold of him, we couldn't manage to track him down. Sometimes this went on for days at a time. He wouldn't answer his phone and even when he was in the office, he was so frantic about catching up on work that he was essentially unavailable for conversations. He came to us when he needed something, but he wasn't physically or mentally present when *we* needed *him*.

Over time, we all began to sense he was keeping us in the dark to hide what he was working on, as he was only interested in our sales results and furthering his own career at our expense. We started to resent him, ridicule his behavior, and silently hope he would fail. This gave me firsthand insight into how destructive too much self-focus in a leader can be for the team.

The second underlying reason for excessive self-focus is also rooted in fear, as mentioned before, but manifests differently on the surface. For some leaders, situations that are new and complex can lead to overwhelm and confusion. They feel unable to get things under control, leading to a lack of confidence and self-doubt. I've heard leaders say, "I actually worry, as I try to deal with problems by myself too often. I don't share my problems because I don't want to burden other people. I tell myself, I have to be resilient. It's my job. My responsibility. I'm supposed to come up with solutions and direction. But I constantly worry if I'm doing enough. Am I doing the right thing?" Part of achieving success is believing you *can* in the first place. Without that faith, you'll end up drowning in anxiety and give off the impression that you can't be trusted.

SELF-CONFIDENCE IN THE MIDST OF UNCERTAINTY

I've seen many leaders who believe they need to show up knowing everything and having all the answers. They derive their self-confidence from their level of knowledge and expertise. In reality, true self-confidence comes from knowing yourself and having the unshakeable belief that you'll be able to handle whatever occurs.

When you're faced with a situation that's new, unpredictable, or triggering for you, don't panic. Instead, think about all the big changes that have happened in your life, the achievements you've earned, and the hurdles you've conquered. They all resulted from periods of uncertainty. There are no "bad" situations, only low-gear thinking *about* situations. Keep in mind that any circumstance you encounter is there for you to approach from high gear. They are an opportunity to learn and grow.

Ask people around you:

- What is happening here exactly?

- What's the opportunity here?

- What can we learn from it?

- What are we NOT seeing that could help us move past this?

- What are the risks?

- What could be the benefits?

Evaluate situations based on facts, not judgments. These are great sources of feedback about the quality of the processes and communication in place.

Focus on People and Behavior Before Content

As you're collecting information during your initial meetings, you may find yourself focusing closely on the technical content of what you learn. As it's not content you can add value to right away, shift your focus toward people and behavior. This isn't just about building trust, but also noticing how people interact with one another.

- How is the team operating?

- What do you notice?

- How well do they collaborate?

- What's the level of trust between them?

- How well are they taking ownership?

- How do they speak or give feedback?

- What's their level of engagement?

Start there!

Umesh shared a fascinating story on how he built trust with people right at the start of his new assignment, which was critical for leading his team in an area where he wasn't an expert in the subject matter. He was working as a Supply Chain Vice President for Hindustan Coca-Cola Beverages. Per his new contract, he became responsible for the entire regional supply chain in Western India, including manufacturing, which was completely new to him at the time.

> "When I started, it was very tricky because I didn't know anything about manufacturing," he told me. "I did, however, have some credibility within the organization. I started

talking about trust, people, and values. My discussions were more focused on the behavioral aspects of the business rather than the functional ones, because I knew I still had a lot to learn in that area. I thought, 'If I'm going to lead this team in a field they know more about than I do, I have to first gain their trust.'"

During his initial team meetings, he put trust on the agenda as his main focus, centering on the importance of values, how people show up to work, and how they communicate.

"I knew that once people trusted me as a leader, it would become much easier for them to open up to me. I wanted to be seen as approachable so people would feel they could come to me. I didn't want them to think, 'He doesn't know manufacturing. Why would I go to him?' Gradually people started to share, and everything came to the surface. Within a month, I had achieved full transparency about the problems my team was having, whether they were people problems, functional problems, or capital problems."

As a result of Umesh's focus on building trust, something remarkable started to occur. As his team began to trust him, they also started to trust each other more. Trust was a conversation they were having as a group.

Despite knowing nothing about the technical aspect of his new role, he was able to move forward. He didn't aim for information or collecting the knowledge he lacked. He also didn't operate according to a hidden strategy he kept to himself. He brought everything out in the open, which was apparently important to the people he was there to lead. Soon, people felt able to approach him with any problem they were experiencing without

fear of repercussions. He then began talking with them individually and giving them clear priorities to focus on.

Naturally, there were some people who had been with the
company for a long time who were reluctant to change their
ways, but he was able to manage them by taking a more personal
approach. He gave them certain responsibilities based on their
seniority in the company, making it known that he was relying
on them and their expertise. This allowed them to feel seen
and valued for what they knew, empowering them in ways that
earned them respect from others. He played the team dynamics
in a way that inspired people to look to each other to learn, get
better at what they do, and take their performance to the next
level. It was the personal connection that allowed them to get
there collaboratively.

Use Your Company Values as a Compass

If you're unsure which direction to take when confronted with
difficult decisions, your company values can be a great source of
direction when decisions have to be made. If you stick to those
values and believe they're important in driving your business
forward, you can make choices that align with them. That's what
they're there for, after all. By using them as your compass, you'll
be able to zero in on what will be best for you and your team at
that moment.

Becoming comfortable with discomfort is your key to navigating the ocean of the unknown. Stepping into a challenging situation admitting to yourself and others that you don't have all the
answers can be very comforting. It also tends to inspire the trust

we seek, as people don't tend to trust people who think they have all the answers. In the next chapter, I'll talk about the risks that come with a know-it-all mindset and how you can avoid being blinded by your own interpretations.

8

TRAPPED IN THE TOWER OF TRUTH

When We Think We Know It All

"The illiterate of the 21st century will not be those who cannot read and write, but those who cannot learn, unlearn, and relearn."

—ALVIN TOFFLER

JOHAN, ONE OF THE CLIENTS I MENTIONED EARLIER, MOVED to the Philippines in his late twenties on his first assignment in Asia. When I asked him about the biggest obstacle he had to overcome during that time, he told me, "I made the mistake of very simplistically thinking what I'd seen work in the US or in Europe would work in other countries without any sort of customization or adaptation. That was my first attempt in the Philippines and it worked very poorly. I was loud and believed that what we had been doing in the US for the past ten years was the only way of doing things. I can't imagine that what I was doing has ever worked for anyone and I spent about a year and a half trying. It's shocking looking back at the fact that it took that long to recognize it, but I guess that's part of being inexperienced with working in foreign countries. It was the hardest lesson I've ever had to learn, but I'll never forget it, nor will I ever make that mistake again."

We often don't hear the stories from leaders who admit they've completely ignored the local nuances of their new environment and as a result get frustrated by the lack of progress. Bret, the retired financial executive I mentioned earlier, told me a similar story.

"This happened to me. I worked for Citigroup for nineteen years in North America, in Asia, and I lived in Japan for six years. I was a superstar. So, I got contacted by Barclays Bank in the UK. I took the job because the promise was that I'd be leading a team of 2,000 people. I'd never had a leadership role that big. I stepped in, and after thirty to sixty days, nobody was responding to me. And for the first time in my career, I was scared to death. None of the things I'd done over the course of my nineteen-year career were working. I had not learned to connect with people in a way that built trust, so that was a very hard lesson to learn. Now, I have to give myself a little bit of credit here. I did admit my stupidity and the fact that there was so much I did not know, and that helped a lot because I was willing to learn. I sought out professional support and luckily responded well to it. It was a lot of hard work, but it paid off for me professionally for the ten or so years of my career that followed, for my personal wealth and for the business. My value in the marketplace increased exponentially when I figured out how to connect with others and build trust. I learned to engage with people on a personal level so I could help them develop and grow, as I then understood their personal needs. This type of talent is not in abundance. Therefore, the market was willing to pay a premium for it."

Both Johan and Bret had gotten trapped in what I call the tower of truth. This can happen when we step into a new role thinking we know it all and, as a result, end up getting completely stuck. In this chapter, I'll discuss how you can find the exits.

WHAT'S THE CHALLENGE?

Getting stuck in the tower of truth often happens to leaders who have been working in an organization longer and step into a new role in a different part of the world, or move from headquarters to one of their local subsidiaries. If you find yourself in this situation, you may assume, or may even see it as part of your assignment, that you should run projects exactly as people did in your previous organization, role, or country. Chances are you've been offered your new role because of your experience and because you know everything about the business. It seems to make sense that to be successful, all you need to do is carry the strategies, processes, and systems you used in the past into your new environment. You may believe that because you know how things work, it's your role to teach and tell, and everyone *else* in their host country must listen, learn, and execute according to your vision. The reason that approach fails is that instead of spending time connecting with people and learning about the context already present within the company, you fail to recognize the need or added value of involving your local team in your plan for the mission.

You would not be the first person to think, *There's nothing anyone here can tell me that I don't know already.*

The consequences of getting trapped in the tower of truth are detrimental to everyone. When people aren't being heard or involved in the process, they won't commit to your vision. They won't be inspired to take ownership or accountability for what they're asked to do. In the modern world where demand for top talent is high, those who can afford to do so will leave for greener pastures. The ones who stay will simply be carrying out orders to earn a salary. Your relationship with them will be transactional at best. When things go wrong or your attempts end up failing, they won't feel responsible because none of what happened was their idea to begin with. They may even become cynical and silently hope the project will fail just to prove a point.

"We knew this was going to happen, but you didn't want to listen to us."

BEHIND THE CHALLENGE: COMPETITION OVER COLLABORATION

Leaders who get trapped in the tower of truth aren't necessarily authoritative drill sergeants shouting orders, as you might imagine. I've met many who were kind, well-intentioned people who nonetheless found themselves hitting this particular wall. What these leaders have in common is that they're carrying around beliefs that are making them ineffective in their new foreign environment. These beliefs make them unable to see their new reality for what it is. They don't all share the same beliefs, but there are a few I'd like to mention that tend to be present in these cases.

- They were chosen for their role because they had more knowledge and experience than everyone else who applied. Therefore, to them, adding value means showing they know more than everyone else. They feel a strong need to keep that image alive. In striving for this, they hold their knowledge close to their chest, not wanting to give away what previously made them stand out. They don't involve others in their decision-making because if they involve people who happen to know more or have better ideas, they'll appear to have failed at their job.

- They believe their team members are their workforce and are employed to carry out their plans. They set goals, then their people execute. This belief often comes from having worked in environments that adhere to old-school, autocratic leadership styles with strong hierarchical structures where the leader makes decisions alone or within a small group. They mainly focus on results and expect their team members to do exactly what they ask them to do.

- They believe they are "the creators of their own success." People who have been successful for a long time may have surrounded themselves with people who agree with everything they say. Over time, they lose people who are willing to challenge or disagree with them. They stop receiving honest feedback and constructive criticism. As a result, their ego grows to an extent that they only want to see and hear information that aligns with or confirms their way of thinking. They end up in a bubble where they're unable to perceive reality as it is, separate from the rest of the world.

- They think, "I know the right way of doing things. If people can't do it perfectly, it's better that they don't do it at all. I'll do it myself." These leaders are perfectionists with high standards for themselves and others. Since it's hard to meet those standards, they get frustrated and disappointed with themselves and others for not living up to them. They are often nervous that others will mess up or make mistakes. Often, these kinds of leaders work overtime to make up for the "sloppiness and laziness" of others. This creates anxiousness in the team as well. They begin to doubt themselves and believe their work will never be good enough.

Leaders who hold one or more of these beliefs see the world through a competitive lens: "There's me, and there's them. I am right. They are wrong. Things are black or they're white. I either win or I lose (and I can't let that happen)." When things don't go their way or meet their expectations, they get frustrated and shift into reverse gear, which quickly leads to interpersonal conflicts with the people they should be collaborating with. They blame others or the situation at hand. This way of seeking results creates unsustainable levels of tension, both for themselves and the people around them. People with this type of competitive mindset can indeed be successful, but always at the expense of others, including their team. Those under them become demotivated, disengaged, fearful, and dissatisfied with their work.

I've come to realize that these leaders' competitive mindsets are often a deeply rooted fear of failure. In most cases, the successful track record they built in their home country or former organization was based on their expertise, not their leadership skills. When they're promoted to their new role based on that expertise, they're confronted with a new team that knows nothing about them and likely has a history of handling things differently. The social dynamics at play make it difficult for the new leader to make changes. Rather than focusing on the people they're responsible for, they double down and keep their attention on what they know. They focus on systems, processes, and tasks instead of building trust, inspiring, and engaging people.

There was a senior project manager I worked with in Asia who had moved there from Germany and encountered many difficulties communicating with his team. At his previous company back home, he'd been very successful thanks to his profound technical knowledge, which had earned him high levels of trust, credibility, and success. That knowledge had given him confidence to accept a new role in Asia in a new organization. Right from the start, his focus was on gathering information and learning every detail about the project. To him, this was the logical step. He believed information is knowledge. Knowledge is what brought him success previously. He often shut his office door to avoid distractions, trying to learn everything there was to know about the project he'd been assigned, its history, and all the aspects around it.

As this was happening, his team made no progress. Complaints and problems increased, along with pressure from management for results. Soon he was completely overwhelmed. He became a control freak, setting high expectations for his team and interacting with them in demanding ways, micromanaging them in a tone that clearly conveyed his lack of trust in their abilities. In return, they didn't trust him either, and arguments began to arise frequently. When he couldn't get his way, he locked himself in his office, blaming himself for everything that had gone wrong. He didn't reach out to anyone for help. Instead, he simmered in despair, thinking he had to be resilient no matter what occurred.

"This is *my* job. I *have* to make this work."

This manager, trapped in his tower of truth, didn't need to gather more information, but to start working with his people. Some leaders who decline to do so never manage to progress and can only watch as their project falls apart.

HOW TO OVERCOME THE CHALLENGE

There are a handful of things you can do to avoid getting stuck in the tower of truth (or find your way out if you're there already).

Be Humble

Being the smartest person in the room is not your role as a leader. No leader will ever be smarter than the combined intelligence and experience of their team. Leading with humility and inviting others to share their views will stimulate higher levels of thinking, creativity, learning, and engagement.

Some people think humility involves having a lack of confidence or low opinions of oneself. The reality is that humility revolves around having the self-awareness to understand that putting your ideas, opinions, achievements, and experience above those of others makes it impossible to build genuine relationships. It drives people away. Being humble is about being comfortable with who you are and what you're capable of while appreciating the fact that we all have our blind spots and areas we can improve upon. You may believe humility is incongruent with ambition and determination to achieve success, but that's not the case at all. It just means recognizing that achieving success is not about *you*. Your success and your team's success are one in the same. You cannot have one without the other.

There are a couple of ways you can practice humility. First of all, shift your focus away from yourself and direct it toward other people. Notice what they're doing well. Compliment them and acknowledge their achievements. Every person and situation you encounter offers an opportunity to learn something. Try to find out what that is instead of being quick to judge them based on what you already think you know.

Another path to becoming more humble is to gain a better understanding not only of your strengths, but also your weaknesses. Start owning your imperfections so you can gather the right people to help you fill those gaps. Sometimes what looks like intensely high self-esteem can in fact be linked not with confidence, but repressed negative emotions toward oneself. Some people, as a response to traumatic events, have learned to push those feelings down throughout their lives. In cases like these, it can be helpful to seek support from a psychologist. Traumatic events in our past can make us insecure, causing us to develop large egos as a survival mechanism. Rather than viewing this behavior as a personality problem, understand it is learned behavior that can be changed.

A third path for practicing humility is to practice *asking* rather than *telling*, which I talked about in Chapter 5. Come up with creative ways to shift your conversations by asking people questions rather than telling them what to do.

"What are some other ways you could handle this?"

For more examples of questions you can ask, look back to those given in the Grow phase to help you have conversations that develop people.

Stop Taking Things Personally

Success is the result of a *team* process. If results are different from what you wanted or expected, don't view them as a sign of personal failure. The outcomes you achieve are a reflection of the process, not a reflection of your self-worth.

A result or outcome is merely a neutral situation. It doesn't have any feelings. Understand that when you see results as a sign of failure, that's an indication that you're taking things too personally. The same goes for the feedback other people give you. You may feel frustrated when you hear it, but feedback, if given the right way and well-intended, will provide you with an opportunity to improve the way you do things. This way, you're optimizing your process so it has a greater chance of success.

You may receive feedback that sounds like criticism or a personal attack, and the person giving it may indeed give it with those intentions. Even if they do, there's still no reason to take that personally. They're seeing the situation through *their* lens, not *the* lens. When people intentionally criticize you, they're projecting a reflection of the low gear in which they're operating. It has nothing to do with you. If you take things coming from people who are out to hurt you personally, you fall victim to their reality, which will pull you down into the same low-quality level of thinking where they're functioning. Instead, use your power and energy to shift into higher gear and follow your course. Stop taking things personally.

Reduce Distance

The more distance you put between you and your team, the harder it will be to get people to trust you and buy into your vision. This could involve physical distance, like closing the door to your office or spending the majority of time on the executive floor. It may also involve distance created by hierarchies that exist within your organization. Some leaders may, for instance, feel the need to treat their junior and senior partners differently to adhere to the construct behind those labels.

Physical distance can be reduced by reaching out to people, walking around, asking questions, and having in-person conversations. I recommend not inviting people into your office for those conversations, as that can feel intimidating, especially when you're new and your colleagues are still getting to know you. So, ask for input frequently, but go to people and talk face-to-face when possible. If you're collaborating with people virtually, be sure you speak with them frequently. You want to normalize being available to people and creating the sense that you're approachable. When you're approachable, it makes it far easier for others to share ideas, be creative, and have informal conversations rather than just having planned meetings with formal information exchange.

Changing a hierarchical structure that's been in place for decades is not an easy task. However, it's worth exploring your options around the initiatives you can take within your team to flatten that hierarchy and move away from roles that are designed according to title, like junior consultant or senior partner. Hierarchy by title entails a huge risk of people feeling superior or inferior to one another. It puts them in a box that has nothing to do with their talents, capabilities, creativity, or potential. Great leadership isn't about titles, but about creating an environment where people feel safe to share knowledge and ideas without judgment or fear of punishment. An environment where the best idea counts, regardless of who came up with it.

You might consider defining the roles of your team members around the value they add or the responsibilities they take on. You may have an Investor Relations role, a Digital Media role, or Retail Clients role. Don't label people based on their level. Drop the junior, senior, or principle add-ons so people become less identified with titles. In truth, they have nothing to do with people and the value they bring to the organization.

Knowing Is the Enemy of Learning

Sometimes being more knowledgeable leads to closed-mindedness. Having experience isn't always an advantage. It can narrow our perspective rather than broadening it, leading to less innovation and lower performance. How can you keep your mind open to the fact that there are multiple ways to approach a decision or task?

Tom Chi, a founding member of Google X and former head of product experience at Google, said, "Knowing is the enemy of learning." When we know something, we assume we have the right answer and there's nothing more to explore. This makes learning impossible. Knowing will keep you stuck in your personal bubble. How can you create new levels of success and solve tomorrow's problems when you're stuck in the mindset of being an expert just because you knew how to solve *yesterday's* problems?

Most successful leaders are fully aware that they cannot know everything, nor will they have to. The more we break down the barriers we've created for ourselves, the more we're able to get out of our own way. We'll be more willing to learn from others and equip our teams to tackle tomorrow's challenges through innovative thinking.

In this chapter, we've covered how we can use our authority to lead while ensuring we don't get too wrapped up in ourselves. But what happens when we're tasked with leading without authority? How can you still get results and influence people? Next, I'll talk about how you can get creative in these situations.

9

UNRAVELING THE THREADS OF HIERARCHY

Asserting Influence across Network Constructs

"The first and most important choice a leader makes is the choice to serve, without which one's capacity to lead is severely limited."

—ROBERT K. GREENLEAF

THESE DAYS, MORE AND MORE ORGANIZATIONS ARE SHIFTING from a top-down hierarchical approach toward more collaborative leadership styles. Business authors Ibarra and Hansen define collaborative leadership as "the capacity to engage people in groups outside one's formal control and inspire them to work toward common goals despite differences in convictions, cultural values, and operating norms."

At some point, you may step into a new role that requires you to lead more laterally. Instead of managing projects and making sure goals are achieved, you may have to work alongside your employees while collaborating with other teams and departments to achieve common objectives. The benefits of this collaborative leadership style are increased creative and innovative thinking, open communication, more employee engagement, and better team performance. The team operates under the mentality that everyone is there to tackle challenges and problems together.

There are a number of reasons why organizations decide to incorporate a more collaborative leadership style into their business model. First of all, it breaks down silos and rivalry, as managers, executives, and teams have a shared responsibility to achieve common goals and will therefore more easily share information. Secondly, Millennials and Gen Z will soon comprise the most prominent group of employees in the workplace. They are the world's future leaders. They want to drive change and make an impact, and the red tape created by top-down power structures stops that from happening. The third reason is that increased business complexity requires change that involves people from multiple divisions, functional areas, and sometimes external partners. Traditional leadership structures and boundaries don't fit with this complexity anymore.

To align with this modern approach to business, you may need to influence people without formal authority. In this chapter, I'll discuss how you can unravel the threads of hierarchy while still leading effectively.

WHAT'S THE CHALLENGE?

Adapting to a network-based leadership model will require you to develop a different skillset than leading from the top down. You won't have formal authority as an individual, therefore you'll have to create a collaborative network by developing strong relationships, building trust, and being an effective communicator.

Very few senior leaders have been trained to lead collaboratively. Most of us developed our leadership skills by copying the leadership styles of the people we were once led by, who likely had a more traditional style. It makes sense that you might have difficulty finding your place within this new modern structure. I've spoken with people who literally told me, "I feel lost." They felt impatient and wondered, "How will I manage to get things done in this type of environment?" In the past, they had clear playbooks for how to do things based on hierarchical lines, experience, and their personal network. Those playbooks are no longer relevant.

Now we must learn to effectively influence rather than manage. You may need to use resources located elsewhere in the organization, outside of your own department or location. Work may be done more globally than before. Resources may be more centralized. Therefore, working toward common goals means putting the overall organization's goals and priorities over your own. Where in the past, leaders were champions at speed skating, they're now suddenly asked to play ice hockey. The rules of the game have changed.

Not all modern organizations are making this shift, but it's bound to become more common over time, particularly in tech-related businesses. Even if you don't see this happening at your organization, you're likely to get involved with collaboration-based organizations in your supply chain or among your customers where you'll be required to apply your influencing skills. Leading laterally is an increasingly fundamental aspect of leading globally. You're bound to have to influence people across multiple geographic locations. Additionally, in the context of the War for Talent that developed during the COVID-19 pandemic, more organizations are looking to fill their talent and skill gaps. When those gaps can't be filled by people already on the payroll, external organizations and contractors must be incorporated to get the job done. This can entail adding consultants or freelancers to your project network, who set their own policies and will not automatically align with your organization's rules and regulations. Keeping all of this in mind is essential.

BEHIND THE CHALLENGE:
A DESIRE FOR CONTROL

Typically, there are two types of leaders who find leading without authority challenging. The first are those whose success was built upon their personal achievements in their network, where they had a respectable reputation. They used to be the smartest people in the room. They identify strongly with their role, their title, and the status that comes with that. When their title or position loses importance (in their eyes, at least), they can experience a loss of identity.

Effectiveness now depends on how well you maneuver in a more networked organization. Success now depends on how easily you can shift from "me and my team" to "us and the organization."

How easily can you let go of control and step into a new type of power that's less overt?

The second type of leader who tends to have trouble leading without authority is someone who's used to making decisions that align perfectly with their personal values. In more collaborative work environments, they find that their views and opinions are challenged and questioned more often. Compromise becomes necessary if they're to come to a decision. They see their vision being diluted by other people's ideas and feel their values are being sacrificed.

I once worked with a global creative director who led advertising campaigns for a number of famous brands. Creativity was one of his core values. He didn't take it lightly. When his organization shifted to a network-based structure and he started his new advertising role, he felt that because they were a market leader, their branding campaigns had to be first-class masterpieces, thereby setting a new standard for success. He aimed to provoke emotion through stunning commercials. He wanted the most innovative, powerful, mind-blowing campaigns in his field. In the new organizational structure, he had to work in a more collaborative environment with people from other functional fields. Some found his advertising concepts to be too wild, extreme, or different. At times, they chose campaigns he couldn't agree with. Having to take everyone's opinions into account made him frustrated and angry, as if his values were being violated. In his eyes, creativity was not a democratic process.

This leader was stuck in a values conflict. He began to doubt whether he had made the right choice stepping into his new role. Staying 100 percent true to his values could result in a reputation of being too rigid. Yet, he enjoyed the fact that he had huge growth opportunities and took part in leadership development programs that came with the role. Eventually he found a way to combine his values, not having to compromise at all, and found new ways to express his creativity. He would never have gotten there had he not come to terms with the fact that the organization was moving away from developing champions to building strong networks.

HOW TO OVERCOME THE CHALLENGE

Let's talk about skills you can use to unravel the threads of hierarchy without getting stuck. How can you influence others without authority?

Connect, Serve, Receive

Just as you did during the Connect phase described in Chapter 3, start by using the Connect Card to map out the people who will be the most important to form relationships with. Whose help will you need to accomplish your project's goals? Who will be impacted by the changes you want to make? What knowledge and expertise do you have in your current network? What gaps exist in the areas of creativity, innovation, technical skills, or market expertise? How can you expand your network to get your project up to speed quickly? You'll need to build a wide network with a variety of people across and outside your organization, depending on where the gaps are.

Next, it will be important to find ways to help and serve your stakeholders *before* approaching them about helping you. Ruth, who I mentioned before, for example, was a Supply Chain Planning and Group Logistics Director. In her role, people weren't reporting to her and she had no direct line of authority with them. This shaped the way she worked with them.

"I have what I call an 'emotional bank account' with people. It's a give-and-take relationship and I'm very mindful not to always be taking," she told me. "I always ask myself, 'What have I done for them today? I make mental checklists and make sure I provide value to them before asking for something. I work with large teams, but I'm mindful not to send out too many group emails. I will never ask people for things as part of a group email. Instead, I take a more personal approach and ask for specific things in an individual. personalized email. Again, I'm building a relationship that is personal, instead of them feeling they are one of many. I'm intentional when I contact certain people to ensure I provide something that helps them, before asking them for something in return."

Be Curious and Listen

You want to be curious about what goes on in other people's worlds in order to lead without authority. If you ask questions and express genuine interest in others, they'll open up and tell you more about what's important for them. They'll share their struggles, aspirations, and visions for what they'd like to see happen in their work environment. Listen carefully for specifics about what's going on for them. Learn so much about them that you know how they think so you can imagine what life is like from their point of view. This will give you insight into how you could serve them, and it will help you build trust, which will be necessary if you're to influence people.

Below are forty questions you can ask that will make people feel you genuinely care about them and what's important to them. These questions can be used in discussions with external stakeholders, and you can easily adapt them when talking to internal stakeholders as well.

Questions to ask about business:

1. What do you want me to know about your organization?

2. What drives your business forward?

3. Paint me a picture of what the future of your organization looks like.

4. What is your vision for the business?

5. What are your future goals?

6. Where is the company today?

7. What essentially needs to happen to bridge the gap between the two?

8. What are you most concerned about when it comes to growing your business?

9. What's the impact you're trying to make as an organization?

10. What role does your division/department/team play in the organization?

11. How do you see your division/department/team progressing?

12. Tell me about your company culture and values.

13. Why do people like to work in your organization?

14. What do people appreciate most about working here?

15. Why do people tend to leave your organization?

16. What needs to stay in place if you're to be/remain successful?

17. What needs to change if you're to be/remain successful?

18. What are some important market developments at the moment?

19. What are the internal/external challenges you face?

20. What are the internal/external opportunities available to you?

21. What other important factors influence the future success of your organization?

22. What is your reputation as an organization?

23. What is your reputation as a division/department/team?

24. Why do customers buy your products/services?

25. How are your products/services perceived in the market?

26. What do your customers value most?

27. What are your customers complaining about?

28. What sets you apart from the competition?

29. How are you tracking your results?

Questions to ask about their relationship to you:

1. How do you work with partners/suppliers?

2. What happened in cases where partner/supplier relationships failed in the past?

3. What would you like to see happen if we worked together?

4. Where can we make the biggest difference for you?

Questions to ask about their needs:

1. What results are you looking for when it comes to...?

2. Why is changing the way you work regarding...so important to you?

3. What does a successfully completed [project] look like to you?

4. What's the best possible result of us working together?

5. What's the worst possible result of us working together?

6. How will you know that our product/service will have worked for you?

7. What are the specific criteria you'd measure us against to see whether we and our products/services have been successful or not?

Getting the answers to these questions will provide you with the information you need to serve your stakeholders and be truly influential.

Serving Is Different from Pleasing

Now that you know what could make a difference for your stakeholders, start helping them. Where could you and your team make a difference for them? Helping is an act of *service* we perform by adding value. Serving them is not the same as pleasing them. I've talked with many leaders who seem to confuse the two.

Striving to please others is backed by a desire for everyone to like and approve of you. Many leaders who are pleasers develop time-management problems due to their habit of taking on other people's problems in addition to their own. If this is you, you might feel good about solving people's problems, and many will be more than happy to accept your support. In such cases, you say yes to too many people but don't end up influencing them.

People pleasers are often on a fast path to burnout as they work incredibly hard to gain recognition and acknowledgment. They need that validation from others to feel successful. But the stress of taking on more than we can realistically handle keeps us from making progress on our own mission. Being focused on pleasing others can also harm our credibility and reputation. It can come off as "sucking up." Some people may even take advantage of us and instead of building trust with them, we start resenting them—the opposite of what we want to achieve.

When you focus on serving rather than pleasing, you become more influential in ways that add greater value for others. You don't have to be liked by everyone to achieve this. You want to make an impact, serve the organization, and serve other people in a way that adds value as you do something they wouldn't be able to accomplish otherwise.

Get clarity before helping people out by asking yourself two questions:

- Am I serving or am I pleasing?

- Where am I adding value?

I recently spoke with a leader who was having difficulty at work because he didn't realize he was pleasing rather than serving. The CEO of his company, which is based in Europe, had assigned him an operations role in Asia, where business hadn't been running smoothly. My client's role was to support the current managing director, who had been promoted from a sales role and needed managerial support. Unfortunately, this managing director saw my client as a threat to his position rather than an asset and kept him at arm's length, only passing along small projects and assignments that didn't shift the needle much at all. The leader got frustrated, knowing he wasn't adding value, but still saw it as his responsibility to help the MD. Six months into his role, he hadn't made much progress. This is because progress isn't made through pleasing, only through serving.

How can we serve rather than please in these situations? In my client's case, it would be building a relationship with the managing director in a way that creates trust rather than fear. That trust would allow for more openness and space for difficult conversations that involve challenging how things are done and experimenting with new approaches that can lead to new insights and different outcomes. Because of my client's desire to please, he allowed the MD to keep him busy with surface-level work and conversations, diverting his energy away from the core problems the organization had. Once my client started serving instead of pleasing, he started taking another approach. He shifted away from the need to be liked and focused on the company's survival. His approach became more powerful when he said to the MD, "We have to work together or the organization won't have a future here in Asia. We have to *serve* the company and therefore change the way we do things here."

Commit and Keep Your Word

Helping others in the ways you say you will is key to influencing without authority. It sounds simple, but it's actually surprisingly rare. Be careful about what you commit to and be conscious of the language you use when you're making promises. Making promises you can't keep damages trust and ultimately leads to confusion, or worse.

People often say, for instance, "Let's meet next week" or "Let's discuss this next time" when they have no real intention of doing so. In some cultures, expressing those empty intentions is viewed as a way of being polite. However, it creates disappointment, frustration, and eats away at your reputation when you don't follow through. Trust is difficult to gain, but easy to lose. Keeping commitments imparts power because things get done. Progress actually gets made, which builds credibility and trust.

Create a Collaborative Environment

Influencing those we work with when we lack formal authority requires a collaborative environment. We must also help the people on our projects find their way around the network of the organization. How can you do this in a way that makes people feel supported and welcome to contribute?

First off, be vocal and clear about the shared purpose of the organization. Remind everyone of what you're trying to achieve together. Communicate this message often as a reminder that everyone is working toward common goals. Ensure that everyone understands how they're expected to contribute so they can see which piece they're adding to the puzzle. They might be working on something that has no obvious link to the end product, but if they can see the big picture of how their efforts fit together, they'll know that what they're doing matters.

Secondly, be a role model by modeling the behavior you want to see. Provide honest, constructive feedback while seeking the same in return. Open doors for others and encourage them to engage in effective dialogues across functional teams. When they see you having those kinds of conversations and inviting them to do the same, this will embolden them to widen their network as well.

Third, encourage creativity and new ideas for improvement and growth. Take risks and share the knowledge you learn from your successes and failures, as both kinds of input are equally valuable parts of the process. When you do this, you help create an environment of experimentation where it's okay to challenge the status quo.

Finally, share information freely and openly. Be transparent with them about what's happening in the company and how it's affecting the team. If they have this information, they'll again be able to see their place in the bigger picture.

In this chapter, we've covered how you can be effective in leading laterally rather than from the top down. Next, we'll cover what to do when you step into a new assignment and find you've been left with a mess.

10

THE MUDDY QUICKSANDS OF THE PAST

When You're Met With a Mess

"Tolerance is endorsement when failure is ignored."

—ANONYMOUS

OUR WORLD IS CHANGING WITH INCREASING SPEED AS OUR global society evolves. The term VUCA (Volatility, Uncertainty, Complexity, and Ambiguity) has been used over the past few decades to describe the main characteristics of challenges in the business world. This term, however, has taken on new meaning since the beginning of the COVID-19 pandemic. We have additional issues to confront together, like increasing geopolitical tension, rising prices, a lack of resources, and other changes that are impacting businesses all over the world. New developments in the tech world require everyone to adapt at an ever-quicker pace. We and our organizations need and want to be prepared and resilient enough to deal with what comes next.

It's highly likely that the goal of your assignment will involve making fundamental changes to how business is done to help your organization cope with one or more of these challenging market circumstances. Being effective in driving change and having change-management skills as a leader has become essential. The alarming reality, however, according to a McKinsey study, is that 70 percent of change initiatives fail. This is largely due to employee resistance and lack of management support. I also see change programs fail due to lack of leadership skills, resources, and poor planning.

What can you do when you've inherited a mess you weren't anticipating, whatever the reason for it is? This chapter is about how to handle assignments plagued by messes you weren't anticipating on top of the original challenges you've set out to accomplish.

WHAT'S THE CHALLENGE?

In situations where you find yourself stuck in the muddy quicksands of the past, the challenge you face may involve either external parties existing outside your organization, or internal parties involving your colleagues. When the problem is affecting external parties—perhaps revolving around customers or the impact of your products or services on individuals or the public, you'll have to adopt an approach that's specific to the source.

One leader I interviewed, Assad, remembered a challenge he encountered when he began a new role as regional business head at a large organization stationed in the United Arab Emirates.

> "My mission was to grow the business in the Middle East region. After coming from a position involving a smaller market, I was excited about my new opportunity and prepared well for it. I had made a 100-day plan before I landed in the role, but what I found was not part of my plan. I landed in a mess. In my role, I was looking after the distributors, which were huge conglomerates. My company made up less than one percent of their revenue in most cases. We just weren't a big player for them. When I got into the role, I realized that many had pending problems that had gone unresolved for years. Nobody had ever gotten to the core of those problems because people at my company generally moved on every eighteen months or so."

The consequence of this problem was that Assad's distributors essentially hated his company. They didn't want to talk or meet with him. They shut him and his organization out completely. Not a great foundation to work from when your mission is to grow the business.

In cases like Assad's, the essence of the problem boils down to a lack of trust. As I've touched on many times in this book already, we all want to be seen, feel respected, and have opportunities to grow. When one or more of those components are missing for your clients or other external stakeholders, chances are they'll eventually give up on your brand, your products, services, your management, and your company. And if *you* are the new representative at your organization, they'll be giving up on you before you've even started.

You may also encounter internal challenges when you start your new role. These may be problems of a more personal nature. Conflicts between colleagues, perhaps. Mistrust can also come from the failed attempts to make changes by your predecessors who may have taken a toll on people in the internal organization who are tired of yet another change.

When too many changes have been attempted in the past that didn't yield results, it takes a toll on those involved. "Change fatigue" sets in. It's no wonder they'll feel resistance to the ideas of yet another new manager attempting a fresh approach. They're likely exhausted from adopting changes associated with new technologies, organizational restructuring, and culture initiatives.

Stepping into an environment where those before you failed—relationships have been lost, trust has disappeared, and employees are tired of change—requires a different approach. First, you'll need to look a bit deeper to discover what's really going on. How could your predecessors have let this happen? If you find out what occurred before you arrived, you can discover the root cause of why solid ground turned to quicksand.

BEHIND THE CHALLENGE: AVOIDANCE AND A LACK OF TRANSPARENCY

There are two main reasons leaders don't end up effectively dealing with problems they inherit from the past.

Avoidance

Leaders tend to be focused on the future and don't like looking backward. They may have been aware of the issues they were neglecting, but were afraid of opening Pandora's box and being unable to handle what might come out. Some problems have considerable legal and financial implications impacting the company's reputation. Some leaders fear addressing issues that may develop into conflicts with internal or external stakeholders, meaning there's a risk of the issue becoming public—something they will want to avoid at any cost.

No leader is comfortable having these kinds of issues happen on their watch, as they can damage their career or potentially stagnate, derail, or overshadow their performance, or the results they're trying to achieve. It may have felt easier to ignore, divert away from, or downplay the importance of *real* issues than facing and trying to solve them. "Let's focus on the positive and move on to get results."

At best, rather than solving the issue, leaders may have "managed" the situation to minimize negative impacts and keep things moving forward. This is because they're results oriented, not process oriented. What is avoided does not go away; it festers. This will stop them from building deeper relationships and damage trust, as others won't be sure what else they may be hiding.

Lack of Transparency

If you take on a new role at a company where there's no open, honest, straightforward information-sharing on important matters, you'll likely find team members who feel uninformed, disengaged, and less willing to trust you or management in general. The result of these scenarios is that people feel frustrated, mentally check out, or do the bare minimum.

Martin once told me during our interview about a mess he encountered that arose from a lack of transparency. He was working as the management director of the company's global capacity center in India, primarily with operations in engineering. His organization had large growth ambitions, but when Martin got started, he quickly discovered trust in the management team was absent.

"My predecessor had been assigned to lead operations by the COO, but had zero relevant engineering experience. There had been other managers in line for that role—ambitious managers with solid engineering backgrounds who felt they'd been bypassed completely. They didn't understand why the COO had made the decision to hire someone they saw as unqualified. By the time I stepped in, that COO had already left the company, but I still had to lead the people on the management team who had been individually competing for my role. It was a complete mess."

HOW TO OVERCOME THE CHALLENGE

You don't want to become the next leader in line to leave your team in shambles. How can you regain the right people's trust and get buy-in for your plan?

Get the Facts

When you start to find out about misdoings that happened in the years before you arrived, the first thing to do is press the pause button and get to the bottom of what's happening. This can feel counterintuitive when you've got a big mission to accomplish in a limited amount of time, but you need to know the facts before moving forward. You don't want to risk being confronted with more surprises, which can come in the form of complaints, claims, or facts you wish you knew earlier. Investigate the issue thoroughly to find out everything you can. If there are multiple issues, try to compartmentalize them so they're easier to prioritize.

You can make this investigation your first project and be transparent about it. Begin this process by creating a separate Connect Card in addition to the one you filled out in Chapter 3. The project goal for this card is to clean up whatever has gone wrong. Start connecting with everyone who has been impacted or has knowledge of the matter. Be upfront about why you want to talk with these people and listen to what they have to say without judgment. If external stakeholders are involved in the problem, like clients or suppliers, start internally to get the facts before connecting with them. If harm was done to a customer, you'll need to be well prepared and ensure you know all the facts before meeting with them to make things right.

Show Compassion

When you meet with people who have been negatively affected by the problem at hand, be aware that you're representing management, or if they are external, the organization that caused them harm. The fact that you're a new leader with the best of intentions is irrelevant. You're likely to hear a lot of opinions colored by strong emotions. People's thinking may be stuck in reverse gear. You'll have to separate their feelings from the facts to avoid being dragged into the drama. That doesn't mean you should ignore or be immune to people's feelings. On the contrary, it's best to meet them with compassion, without having to choose sides. Acknowledging where people are coming from goes a long way in mending severed ties.

"I see that this situation has really impacted you."

"I can hear how upsetting this whole thing has been for you."

"No wonder you feel the way you do."

"It makes complete sense that you would be angry/upset/disappointed about this."

Validating another person's emotions doesn't necessarily require you to agree with their interpretation of what's been happening. Their emotions are real, but the reality may still be different from how they experienced it. Still, show compassion, demonstrating that what they're feeling matters to you.

Focus on What You Can Control

You may begin to feel overwhelmed by everything that's going on, as if you're being sucked down into those muddy quicksands yourself. There may be a lot of tension, making you feel like the situation is out of your control. It's important to focus on what you *can* control so you can keep your mind clear.

In your control:

- Your response

- What you say and how you say it

- Where you draw the line

- How you spend your time

- What you focus on

- The goals you set

- Staying physically fit

- Having someone to talk to

Out of your control:

- Other people's opinions about you

- Other people's actions

- What happened in the past

- What will happen in the future

- The results of your efforts (remember, you can only control the process, not the outcome)

Bottom line: don't waste your time and energy on what's out of your control. Keep your attention on what you have control over.

Accept Responsibility

Once you have a clear picture of what's going on, whether the problems at hand are happening inside or outside the organization, you'll want to openly recognize and accept that it's now *your* responsibility to fix it. You didn't make the mess, but you do have to clean it up. Acknowledge what has been happening with the people involved in the problem. Ideally, apologize for what has happened. We sometimes have to be careful with apologizing because admitting to certain mistakes can have legal consequences. In those cases, you can still express *regret* for what's been done so people can hear they're being recognized and taken seriously. They need to hear that their pain is not just seen, but valid.

Own the Problem with Transparency

Whatever steps you take to solve the problem, be transparent about what's going to happen next. Ensure that you engage and work closely with the people who were harmed and affected in the past. Sometimes, financial compensation can be enough to restore people's dignity or financially solve the issue. That may not be enough, however, to rebuild trust. If people have an opportunity to play a part in creating the solution, this will restore trust much more quickly, as they'll feel seen, heard, and valued. When that's not possible, make sure you at least communicate frequently and openly about the steps you're taking and why you're taking them. Transparency is what's been missing in the past. People have to experience that you will do things differently. Check in regularly to hear how your plans for change are being experienced.

Let's get back to Assad. His distributors didn't want to talk with him when he entered his role because they'd been promised compensation for investments they made and were never paid.

"As it turned out," he told me, "we owed them $1.7 million total, distributed over the previous three to four years."

The first thing Assad did was get a list of all the outstanding approved payments from his predecessors that had not been paid out. It was a huge amount of paperwork that took considerable time. In looking at the list, he realized that in some cases, the distributors were right to complain, but some of their other accusations were debatable.

> "Initially the distributor did not want to see me, but I finally got a message through to them saying that I owned all of these problems and stood by whatever commitments were made by the organization before I arrived. I didn't say I'd pay to resolve them all, but I took ownership over each of those issues. The markets in the Middle East are extremely relationship driven, so this got us off to a better start than expected. They agreed to meet with me, but first I asked my team to have a conversation with their team to ensure the list of problems we put forth matched theirs so there would be complete mutual transparency when we met. My intention going into that first meeting with the distributors was to focus only on *them*. I ensured we only talked about what it was they wanted from me. The distributors spent that first meeting airing their emotions, expressing their lack of confidence that anything would change."

"You people come and go," they told me. "You'll be gone in a year and we'll be giving this same story to someone new."

Assad stated clearly that whatever his organization had said in the past, he was now their proxy. Over the course of several additional meetings, he met with the CFO. Again, his organization was a very small player for them, but they started to see him as a fair and equal partner. They were able to come to a mutual agreement when Assad ended up paying $600,000, making the situation transparent by saying he had paid it out of his own P&L, without any provisions.

> "The distributor really appreciated that and it completely turned around how we worked together because we won their trust back. It took us about three weeks and we got over four years' worth of backlog. Our company ended up becoming a preferred partner, leading to a 360-degree turnaround in our relationship and in our business."

Assad's willingness to own the problem with full transparency completely mended that broken relationship.

Make People Part of the Solution

In Assad's example, he got the buy-in of the distributor through transparency, commitment, and making the distributor *part* of the solution. He chose not to take the purely "transactional" approach, which may have been to just pay them out, but chose the "relationship" approach instead to see what he could do for them first.

When there are muddy quicksands *inside* the organization, the same relationship-based approach applies: get the facts and accept responsibility for "solving" the issues. The best way to get buy-in is to make people part of the solution. You don't have to plan out all the details of your solution. Instead, co-create a strategy with the people involved to make sure their needs are heard and empower them to find a common solution. Brainstorm ideas, assess the pros and cons, and decide on the best route. Create plans to put the solution into practice and discuss what resources will be needed over what timescale. Create success metrics and figure out how to monitor progress as well. Consider contingency plans in case the outcome isn't what you're hoping for. Ensure clarity on the roles and responsibilities and get it done as a team.

There will be people who will recognize and appreciate your efforts as you work to solve previous issues. There will also likely be others who see what you're doing as opportunistic or unrealistic. The fear of change may be at play. For some, it will take more time to heal from what has happened. You can't expect to restore trust with everyone immediately, nor can you expect all people to be grateful for your attempt to set things right. Solving an issue doesn't automatically ensure trust is formed. This is natural.

At one point in my career while I was working as a consultant, I was called into an organization to be part of their management task force. We were responsible for restructuring the company, which worked in debt collection and had, ironically, been losing money over time. It was our job to map out the business's processes and propose a total process redesign that aligned with the company's new vision. A few weeks into the role, it became clear that the numbers we were working with weren't accurate. The reports and data we received were produced by an IT system that was over twenty years old. The company had never invested in system updates or maintenance. The IT team had tried to make it work with all types of system workarounds and manually created reports, which led to inaccuracies and errors.

As we soon discovered, the company's financial situation was even worse than we'd originally thought. The IT team didn't want to work with us initially and the reason for that was fear. They were losing their power. In the past, the organization had relied on them for business data and reporting. Their knowledge of the system made them powerful, as nobody aside from the IT team knew how to work the system.

Now, they were expecting to be blamed and possibly fired for the mistakes of their reporting system. Even if that wasn't the case, there was still a good chance the company might decide to eventually replace the system altogether and render their positions redundant.

Step by step, my team and I made it clear that we were there to support rather than blame them. In fact, we *needed* them. They had an important role to play in our process redesign. Slowly but surely, we gained their trust and co-created initiatives to get the company back on track. We would have never been able to do that if we hadn't been transparent and involved the IT department in coming up with the solution.

Don't Shy Away from Conflict

Despite all of your good intentions, when stakes are high and emotions are deeply rooted, you may find yourself in a conflict. Some conflicts are fueled by strong, heated, visible emotions. Others involve coldness. People withdraw, appear emotionless, and avoid contact with you however possible.

Most conflicts arise as the result of one of three things. First, there are judgments made about the other person, other people, or a specific situation. Secondly, there may be denial of responsibility. People who do this might deny facts, outcomes, or accountability for issues they contributed to. Third, there may be a lack of alignment in values. In those cases, each party makes different choices based on what's important to them.

When conflicts arise, we tend to blame either ourselves or others for what's happening. Sometimes we express that blame, but more often we keep it inside due to fear of escalation. If you find that happening, pause and bring awareness to the quality of your thinking. You are in reverse gear, which means you're standing in your mind's way of its ability to be creative, innovative, or curious. You need all those brilliant capabilities to help you reconnect with others and find a solution. Once you have that self-awareness, you can use the following steps to take the sting out of the conflict and come to an agreement.

1. Remember that no one can make you feel anything. The emotions you're experiencing are real, but they're not being caused by the situation or people around you. They're the result of your thoughts about those things. Shift your thinking back into high gear. You can't control what others say or do, but you can control how you respond. Once you shift your thinking, your emotions will also shift, giving you more clarity with which to make conscious decisions about what to do next.

2. Identify your *needs*. What *need* is not being met? Answer the following questions for yourself:

   • What do I need?

   • Why is that important to me?

- What would be different if I got what I needed?

- What would be the benefits of getting what I need?

- What's the cost of me *not* getting what I need?

3. Calmly ask the other party what they need. The people involved may have already told you, but there are probably underlying desires and drivers that will be important for you to understand. Why is what they need crucial to them? You can ask them the questions under #2 to dig a little deeper.

4. From your conversation, start identifying what you can agree upon. You may set a common goal, like, "We both want to create new plans to optimize our time to market," or "We both want to expand our business in product X in Asia."

5. Express the value of your relationship with the other person. "I really appreciate you taking the time and effort to discuss this, as I believe it's important for our working relationship that we come to an agreement."

6. Listen to learn and let the other person finish. Validate what they said before you start sharing your story. Avoid coming in with preconceived ideas or a preset solution but share where you are coming from.

7. Discuss options to resolve the issue based on both of your needs and stories.

8. When conflicts devolve into personal attacks or become toxic, take a break. This can take fifteen minutes, or it

can take a week. Change the process or get an objective mediator involved.

Turning Challenges into Opportunities

Instead of seeing the situation as a challenge, think about how things would be different if you approached it as an opportunity. You may be dealing with situations that have been painful, disruptive, or exhausting, which may have affected your team deeply and have them feeling a sense of loss or grief. It can be helpful to have conversations about your team identity and realize as a team that the way they were in the past may no longer be serving them.

Who does your team want to be moving forward? How can you work together to avoid the same outcome in the future? Who will you all need to *be* to ensure you can handle what's coming? Who will you need to *be* to add value for your stakeholders?

These kinds of questions move you forward. They offer you an opportunity to revise your team identity, reenergize your people, and redefine your common purpose. For information about how to have these conversations, look back to the Inspire phase I outlined in Chapter 4.

A common source of conflict in the workplace is clashes in generational dynamics. Differences in how generations tend to communicate can create barriers that have little to do with people as individuals. This is another opportunity you can use to your advantage, and it centers around the benefits of diversity within your team. Next, I'll talk about how to tackle issues relating to the dreaded generation gap.

11

SAILING THE WINDS OF CHANGE

Building Bridges across Generation Gaps

"Each generation imagines itself to be more intelligent than the one that went before it, and wiser than the one that comes after it."

—GEORGE ORWELL

DOES THE ERA IN WHICH YOU'RE BORN SHAPE WHO YOU ARE?

By now, you understand that to start leading quickly and effectively, you'll have to work on building trust-based relationships from day one. You need to shift the level of those relationships from transactional or strategic to one of professional intimacy. The reality of the situation is that we don't get to choose our team members. You're likely to find some of your people to be easier to get along with than others. Regardless, you'll be required to connect with everyone.

Culture, which we covered in Chapter 6, is one aspect of engaging people that global leaders frequently mention they find hard to overcome. Another is what they perceive as generation gaps.

A head of corporate banking recently told me, "It's very hard to keep the junior team members these days. There's no loyalty. They fold their arms looking at me like, 'What's in it for me? What do you have to offer?' How do I motivate them? It takes twice as much energy to make sure our plan is heard and understood. Then once they're fully trained, they quit and go work elsewhere. It's exhausting."

Another leader I spoke with, the founder of a FinTech company, said, "Junior people are just not doing a good job. Their work is mediocre. They just don't care and yet, they expect a promotion at the end of the year. When they don't get that, they're disappointed. They don't take any ownership. How can I get them to change their behavior?"

Another leader, a director of regulatory affairs in China, told me, "I have five direct reports on my team, three of whom are Millennials, and they are lying flat. How can I encourage them to be more proactive? They *think* they work hard, but if they don't see themselves promoted within two years, they say, "Why should I work harder?" My two other team members were born before the 1970s. They are reaching a plateau and it's hard to motivate them. They've reached a level where they can't grow anymore, but have five more years before retirement."

The 'generation gap' leaders say they face can relate to challenges in dealing with both younger and older generations. Getting everyone on board with desired changes can feel difficult. Leading a team from a mix of generations and managing the dynamics among them can make it feel even more challenging.

WHAT'S THE CHALLENGE?

You may have up to four different generations working together at your organization. Their life experiences, values, and beliefs are bound to be different and can lead to disagreements or even conflicts. Frustration over this can easily lead us to fall back on common stereotypes.

"Baby Boomers are arrogant and inept with technology."

"Gen Xers are spoiled and only care about making money."

"Millennials are entitled and have unrealistic expectations."

"Gen Zers are lazy and narcissistic."

Just because these stereotypes exist doesn't make them accurate reflections of reality. There's little solid empirical evidence to confirm that the era in which you were born determines how you behave. The stages of development we go through in life, however, can be consistent, meaning that the behavior of a mid-twenties professional today will be similar in certain ways to mid-twenties professionals working thirty years ago. Believing generational stereotypes limits our perception in regard to what our people are actually capable of.

Think for a moment about what would happen if a colleague made assumptions about you based on the year you were born. If you were born in 1975, would you agree that you're spoiled and materialistic? I assume not. You might even get defensive in response. That defensiveness arises from being unfairly judged and labeled. A label almost certainly can't do justice to all the other aspects of who you are. This feeling lands you in reverse mode, possibly causing you to judge whoever's judging you according to *their* age in return.

Once we label someone, it's very hard to look past that label. We adopt a me-versus-them attitude without exploring the root of their behavior and what's driving it.

Another point to keep in mind is that a person's belief system and values are shaped by their life experiences growing up, which take place in a context of social, political, and economic events. The events that happened in the countries where your multicultural team's members grew up are bound to be different. Someone who grew up in the 1990s in China will have had a very different life so far than someone who grew up in the 1990s in France. You, as their leader, won't be able to fully appreciate the unique aspects of the backgrounds that shaped them until you've gotten to hear each of their stories. When you take this into account, it becomes ridiculous to label members of global teams according to when they were born.

BEHIND THE CHALLENGE: ASSUMPTIONS ROOTED IN STEREOTYPES

Generational stereotypes are rooted in assumptions, but have little to no evidence proving those assumptions are actually true. We see what we want to see. Why do we do this?

Typically, we make assumptions when we encounter behavior we can't make sense of. If we're not conscious of our thinking, our minds will quickly work to fill in the blanks. We draw upon our own experiences and beliefs in search of understanding. Our brain saves energy this way. It doesn't have to analyze every new situation from scratch. The risk of making assumptions is that it produces a limited view of what's really going on. We block out other possible ways of interpreting the situation. If we don't spend enough time exploring what may be going on with the other person, we make judgments based on our own perspective alone and solidify them in our minds as truth. This tendency separates us from others and creates distance, which is the opposite of what we're trying to achieve while we're building trust.

HOW TO OVERCOME THE CHALLENGE

The biggest hurdle many organizations face nowadays is attracting and retaining the right people. Many have put their HR teams to work coming up with strategies that align the needs of the company with those of its employees. On one hand, they must incorporate different ways of working to ensure the organization is prepared to tackle the challenges and opportunities present in the rapidly changing business world. On the other hand, they have to take into account the changing needs and aspirations of those who get work done on their behalf. We have to consider what our organization can offer in terms of how employee performance is measured and rewarded, how their people can collaborate, and the development opportunities that are needed to help people grow.

As I mentioned before, people don't usually leave bad companies, but bad bosses. To me, this indicates we as leaders aren't doing a good enough job of connecting, inspiring, and growing our people. If we stop using the generation gap as an excuse for this disconnect, it leaves us with the question of how we can connect our organization's expectations with employee needs.

The easiest answer is to come back to the Connect, Inspire, Grow framework as a means of finding out who employees are and what makes them tick. This is not up to HR, but *you* as the leader. You have to initiate conversations that will help your people feel comfortable opening up and sharing what drives them, what aspects of their life are important to them, and what success looks like for them. What does growth mean for them? How can you support them in that? There are many forces at play in people's lives. What they need now may be different from three years ago or three years from now, so having these conversations on a regular basis is essential.

People also experience life changes based on what's happening in the world. The COVID-19 pandemic, for example, caused people around the world to completely reassess their lives. For many of us, it inspired shifts in our personal and professional focuses. As leaders, we have to take into account more than the aspect of work alone in the lives of our team members. There may be personal elements at play that must be addressed simultaneously.

I worked with a senior consultant who has three young children. Her husband also has an international career, which requires him to travel regularly. What she values most about her job is the flexibility her employer affords her, especially while her husband is away. She's able to form her schedule around her kids and work online from home when she needs to. At this point, she's not seeking career growth. For her, fulfillment lies in balancing her work with her personal life. That will change in a couple of years when her youngest child starts school. Her current needs are temporary, but she's getting them met because her employer knows what's important to her and has adapted to suit her needs.

Workplace flexibility initiatives may work for one person, but not the next. You'll have to customize yours based on the individual needs you learn about through your conversations with your team. Refer back to Part 2 of this book for detailed information on how you can lead those conversations.

People's desires and needs change all the time depending on which phase of their life they're currently in. As you move away from focusing on the generation gap, look for ways to connect with people individually instead. You can say, "Hey, I remember when I was in my thirties. I had a young family and both of us worked full time. How are you handling that? Let's have that conversation. What do you need at this point?"

Their answers will be very different from those of someone who plans to retire in five years, or from someone who comes from a culture where they're expected to care for their elderly parents. I've coached expat leaders who lived abroad who were in the middle of divorces and had difficult decisions to make about structuring their lives in a way that would allow them to see their kids. Never assume you know someone's circumstances based solely on their age.

Meeting changing employee expectations will require a team culture that embraces flexibility and prioritizes employee well-being. HR can do the strategic part, but it's up to you to build the connection. That connection, team culture, and flexibility provides a competitive advantage and will make your team more stable and content. Everyone has something they can teach us, whether they're older, younger, or within our own age group. What can you learn from each of your people? Dig below the surface and find the full extent of what they bring to the table.

12

LEADING THROUGH THE CLOUD

The Dos and Don'ts of Leading Teams Online

"The screen does not stop us from connecting. It provides us a different way to connect."

—ANONYMOUS

WHILE WORKING GLOBALLY, YOU MAY HAVE TO LEAD DISTRIB-uted teams where individuals work in separate geographical locations. In recent years, we've seen more organizations where employees work remotely or follow a hybrid setup. The future of work is likely to continue following this trend, meaning many leaders entering new roles will have to onboard remotely too.

When this is the case, your focus at the beginning of your assignment will be to connect and build trust online. Results from the

2022 Microsoft *Work Trend* survey mentioned earlier stated that 43 percent of leaders cited relationship-building as the greatest challenge of hybrid and remote work. How can you handle this effectively? In this chapter, I'll discuss how you can set yourself and your team up for success when your opportunities to meet face-to-face are limited.

WHAT'S THE CHALLENGE?

As I described in Chapter 3, starting a new global role requires us to build trust with people internally and externally, create a network, engage others, and drive change quickly. Having to do this remotely adds an extra layer of complexity to our first 100 days.

The first issue I'll mention is a practical one, which is time zone differences. When you work remotely, your daytime may be nighttime for those you work with, meaning your emails and text messages will be received while they're off the clock. You may unintentionally plan meetings during those times that rub your team members the wrong way. It can be a challenge to engage everyone when there's little time overlap with which to coordinate work.

You'll also encounter many problems already covered in this book. When it comes to culture, for example, you'll have to familiarize yourself with doing business in new markets. Doing this online can be extra challenging, as you can't always see what's really going on. How are the things you say or do being interpreted? How can you fully understand the local context your team is operating in when you are not physically on the ground?

Another issue is the mutual building of trust, another point we've revisited consistently. Forming authentic connections is crucial to building trust at the beginning of an assignment, but this can feel difficult in virtual or hybrid environments. Trust is important in two ways. You not only want to create mutual trust in each other's reliability, competence, knowledge, and decision-making skills. You also want to create *emotional* trust. You want everyone to feel they can rely on the fact that people care about them and their ideas as well as their difficulties, concerns, and well-being.

BEHIND THE CHALLENGE: A LACK OF SOCIAL CAPITAL

Solving practical issues like time zone differences is straightforward, but those involving culture and trust building require a different approach. The Connect, Inspire, Grow framework still applies here, but *how* we do those things will have to happen differently if we're leading in the virtual world.

When it comes to connecting though, you'll likely have many formal meetings online, and you won't have many informal moments together. In an office setting, employees have chances to chat over coffee, at the water cooler, in hallways, or on the elevator. Those seemingly insignificant moments are key to building social capital, which consists of the benefits that result from the relationships we build within our network that enable us to function effectively. We use social capital when we need help with a project, when we're supporting someone else, or when we're helping people. We also use it to help information flow or create new ideas, allowing teams to get more done and perform better.

Working remotely has decreased our opportunities for building social capital. Microsoft's survey revealed that 59 percent of hybrid employees and 56 percent of remote employees have fewer work-based friendships. People now feel lonelier at work, which leads to health problems, reduced productivity, and turnover. Having virtual coffees with your team members just won't cut it. How can you ensure you spend enough time with them without burning them out?

HOW TO OVERCOME THE CHALLENGE

If you're leading a distributed team online, the deliberate investment you must make to create sustained trust is a lot more significant. As the leader, you're the glue that holds your team together. To do this virtually, you'll have to be very proactive and intentional about who you meet, when you meet, and how you meet.

Connect

As you work through the Connect phase over your first 40 days, you'll have many individual meetings with people who play essential roles in your assignment. The selection of the people you meet with will still be based on how you fill out your Connect Card, and your individual interactions with them. Again, your first online meetings should cover three focal points: getting to know each other's background and story, the challenges and pain points they need help with, and sharing your vision and discussing the aspects of the project they can help *you* with.

What will be different about connecting online will be your challenge of understanding the context of situations from the people you talk to, the market they're operating in, and the people they're dealing with locally. That's the part that's missing when you're located in another part of the world. This means it will be even more important to show up to those meetings in listening mode. You can use the questions listed in Chapter 3, but you'll have to add contextual questions that will give you a fuller picture.

"Tell me what that looks like in your market."

"What does that mean for your clients and suppliers locally?"

"What's different and unique in your market?"

"What's important for you in your market?"

"How do you think this will be perceived in the markets you're working in?"

As you listen to their answers, try to put yourself in their shoes and envision what their situation will look like.

As you share *your* vision and ideas with your people, you will also want to paint them a picture of what you have in mind. You'll have to be exceptionally clear and descriptive about what you want to express. Just as it's important for you to understand the local context of your team members, you'll also need to teach them about yours. Talk about where you're from and how work is done so they can learn about who you are and what's important to you.

You also want to be completely transparent about the approach you're taking in your first few weeks. This is especially important when you're exclusively meeting with people online. They have to know that you'll be spending time with stakeholders, listening and learning from everyone involved in the project, and that you will get back to them to share what you've learned. You'll then get your team together to co-create your plan, always remaining available to them. Tell them about these steps, along with how they can best reach out to you. Despite working virtually, you'll need an open line of communication your team members can use to connect, even when you're not formally meeting with them to discuss work.

Inspire

During the Inspire phase, you'll bring your team together for the first time. The purpose of this meeting is, one, to communicate your vision, two, to share your findings from the Connect phase, and three, to begin creating a new team identity together. This is a lot to cover at once. When this meeting has to happen virtually, make sure you allocate enough time to make your way through it. You're likely to break it up into several meetings.

During the first part of this meeting where you share your findings and observations, you'll want to emphasize your team's commonalities as much as possible. Give everyone a chance to respond and reflect on what they've heard. You'll want to be proactive in making sure every person has a chance to speak. As is the case in the real world, you'll have people virtually who are outspoken along with others who are inclined to hold back. You want to hear everyone in the room, even online.

During the second part of this meeting, as you work to create a new team identity and establish a team purpose, you'll first need to find out who your team members are as individuals and establish who they want to be as a group. In Chapter 4, we covered exercises you can use to accomplish this, which are all easily adaptable for virtual use. The lifeline exercise, for instance, can be prepared before the meeting to save time. The discussion will then move toward what winning as a team looks like. This is where you will co-create the plan and tasks are divided.

The next topic for the team to tackle is "how to engage." This part of the meeting is an excellent opportunity to discuss how you want to engage in the virtual world across different time zones. You'll also want to talk about the nature of the work each individual on your team does and their corresponding needs. Whose roles require collaboration and whose can be done individually? Some people won't require much interaction, while others will need considerably more.

Also think about which areas require flexibility and which would benefit from more boundaries. Do certain people always seem to be working late? If so, what's happening there? Can people get their tasks done on time in spite of time differences? If not, would a more malleable approach make that possible? The answer to these specific questions will be different for every team in every country.

Also discuss which events require your whole team to be together in the same meeting. You may, for example, want everyone present during project kickoffs, brainstorming sessions, or in cases when essential information is communicated.

Examples of team agreements may be around online availability. Can you establish a common time when everyone is available, if need be? You might also discuss attendance. Which team meetings does everyone need to attend? When they can't attend, ensure they can send a substitute. What can you agree on about recording meetings for people who can't make it, but wish to stay informed? Where can you share and store those recordings? How can you protect those files in the same way you protect other important company documents? Also, what agreements might you create about blocking calendars during offtime? There are people who are so protective of their private time that they make it impossible to book meetings with them while they're off. Is this acceptable in the context of your mission or will they need to be more flexible?

There are countless ways you can make working remotely run smoothly. You could, for instance, automate when the emails you write are sent out through the platform you use. That way, the message you wrote at 3:00 p.m. won't pop up in your team's inboxes at 10:00 p.m. Rather than planning meetings back to back, allow a ten-minute break between them. Make agreements about when the team should email versus call or text. What's the expected response time on emails? What about agreements around turning computer cameras on to foster more human connection during online calls? Proactively addressing these questions demonstrates that you respect people's time. You may have to revisit the agreements you make regularly to see whether they're working. The intention behind all this is to care for people's health and build trust. These small steps go a long way in terms of making others feel cared for.

Grow

From around day 80 onward, you'll move into the Grow phase we covered in Chapter 6. During this stretch of your assignment, you'll be holding regular meetings to check in on how things are unfolding. These include team meetings and individual meetings. How can you structure them to ensure you spend time on bonding to generate social capital with your team members and have a productive outcome?

It all begins with good preparation. Be clear about what the objective of each meeting is and have a clear agenda sent to them in advance. If it's going to be a longer meeting, organize topics into ten- to fifteen-minute segments so people stay focused and engaged. If any documents need reviewing, send them upfront so time is spent efficiently on discussions and decision-making only. And finally, make sure everyone is able to connect online. Check that they have all the necessary information, such as links, login details, passwords, and knowledge of how to use the meeting software. This all sounds basic, but you'd be surprised how much time gets lost in meetings due to technical issues.

When it comes to the meetings themselves, whether they're happening on the individual or team level, start by creating space for social engagement. Put eight to ten minutes aside to ask them how they're doing. What's going on with them? How has their week been so far? What's been exciting or difficult for them lately? You can model these online "water cooler moments" by bringing in your own stories to share. This will inspire people to eventually do the same, even if they're from a culture where people are not accustomed to talking about themselves. Make these moments intentional and inclusive. By investing that personal time before diving into the items on your agenda, you'll create stronger bonds.

Denise had a business executive role at an international bank in Hong Kong, leading distributed teams in Australia, Singapore,

Indonesia, and India when COVID hit. She had met most of them in person once, but was forced to continue to work remotely with them from then on as countries went in and out of lockdown.

"This completely changed the way I had conversations," she told me. "When I reached out to people before the pandemic, we would just jump into a conversation right away. 'What are the figures? What's working? What's not working?' Now there was more of a personal introduction every time. 'How are you doing? How's your family?' I got to know people, team members, and business partners so much more closely. Even though we work remotely and we didn't see each other in person, I realized so clearly that knowing people's family situations, what's going on in their lives, can tell us a lot about what's impacting their performance. I'm much more aware of that now. I still consciously take time to ask questions about people's lives, even now when we have the opportunity to see each other face to face, but not regularly. I started to understand people better and how they adapt to change. I also began celebrating some of our small victories during the year and it's great. It keeps morale up. Leading virtually is not an ideal situation for me, but I think I personally grew and learned a lot during that period and how we adjusted to it."

Creating time for people to engage on a personal level leads to greater productivity and team cohesion, better performance, and the ability to work together in the long term. It may feel inefficient, but at the end of the day it improves the relationship you have with your team, as well as the relationships they have with each other. This is an extremely valuable use of your time and energy.

How can you monitor performance online? Truthfully, you can't always monitor individual or team performance closely while working virtually. You may not need to when you have an experienced team. But if your team is relatively new or you don't know them well yet, you'll want to see that they're meeting deadlines, taking initiative, and meeting quality standards independently, without you having to remind them. Make sure, first of all, that the goals are clearly defined. Don't just put your expectations out there, but discuss what needs to be done and get their agreement on the goals, the quality standards, and deadlines. Also, agree on what people will do in the event that deadlines cannot be met, or if access to resources or the scope of work changes. Schedule regular development meetings and "feed-forward" meetings too, just as you would during an in-person Grow phase.

Make sure that your communication is not just outbound by creating ample avenues for others to access you. For example, you might set aside one-hour time slots on Zoom that people can choose to jump into or out of if they wish to. Don't force them to come to these "check-in hours," as that will just be chalked up to another item on their to-do list. Instead, offer them as an open invitation for people to connect with you. They might want to share ideas, report something they're proud of, or ask questions. Sometimes, no one will show up, but other times you can spend that time with a few people talking about anything that's on their mind.

On your end, be sure to communicate with your entire team and the organization regularly. Be seen. Show people what you're up to. Talk about team achievements, next steps, client acknowledgments, or special events. Share what you've learned recently about the market. Make it live and interactive when you can. Alternatively, consider recording short videos with this information that everyone can watch from home each week. The point is that people will want to see who you really are. They want to get to know you and what your style is, how you communicate, and how you make decisions. People like to know what to expect, so don't keep them guessing. Find ways to show them that aren't too time-consuming or intrusive.

Once you have your team's trust, you have to continue to constantly build on it. The virtual world can chip away at trust when there's less connection among people. We have to nurture these bonds and spend time together to keep them strong. Relationships are like fireplaces. You have to keep putting wood on them to keep them burning bright.

FINAL THOUGHTS

"Travel sparks our imagination, feeds our curiosity, and reminds us how much we all have in common."

—DEBORAH LLOYD

As you move into your new global role, you will encounter challenges. Challenges between you and others that you don't understand. I say this is the only challenge you really need to resolve. It provides a hidden key that reveals itself as you first explore and then resolve it. This key is a deeper kind of relationship: the connection from human to human. As long as we blame our challenges on differences in culture, our level of knowledge, personality, language, or age, we deny ourselves the possibility of *real* connection. We won't find that elusive key. It is when we make the effort to connect more deeply, beyond what we want people to do or what makes sense on a purely strategic level, that we can uncover it.

The journey of your new role starts with how well you understand your own mind. How your thoughts create your feelings that determine how you show up in situations. How well you are aware of, understand, express, and regulate your thoughts and emotions. If you have that self-awareness, you can address challenges from a higher level of thinking, resulting in better performance and higher levels of success.

Your journey continues in finding ways to connect with people—team members, clients, board members, and the wider organization who can make an impact or will be impacted by the assignment you are given. This involves approaching them with a service mindset. "How can I help them first?" You want to ask the questions that will make people feel you care and listen to what they tell you about who they are, what they need, and what's important for them.

After that, it's time to get the team together, share your findings, and get them inspired. The team will need to want to do the assignment together with you. They must believe that the future you envision is the right direction, and have faith that they can make it happen. This is also the time when you facilitate conversations to help people connect at a human level, both with you and each other. You want to create a team purpose based on what they value, what they believe in, and what makes them unique as a team.

The next step is to create a plan together with your team. They will need to be part of creating the steps to change. Their opinions and ideas need to be integrated into the rollout of the assignment to guarantee their buy-in. The quicker you have their buy-in, the easier it will be to drive the change for them to be advocates in the wider organization. This all starts with the connection you build within your team. The better they know each other and their perspectives, backgrounds, and values, the more respect and understanding they will have for each other.

How can you keep talented people engaged and on board while they're hunted by other organizations eager to lure them in with high salaries and perks? We know all people want three things. They want to be seen, be respected, and grow. Through the type of connection we build with them, they feel valued and heard. Growing is what all of us want in our lives. Growth in our personal lives and our professional lives. Growth in wealth, knowledge, freedom, fun, and happiness. More growth leads to a fuller expression of life. Providing growth for people in the area they want to grow in will naturally tie them to you.

If you create relationships with people on the human level, you'll know what drives them and what growth and success mean for them. When you know in which aspects they want to grow and are able to provide that, they will value that and return the favor to you with gratitude, trust, and loyalty.

The types of challenges you're likely to encounter during the first 100 days of your global assignment will be different from the challenges you're used to, but not that different. Now you know where to look for the key to solve the issues. When we explore a little deeper, the key to solving them is found in how we connect with people, how we inspire them, and help them grow. I would dare say, in fact, that any problem you experience in relationships can be solved by investing time and attention in building connections.

They say travel broadens the mind and I fully believe this is true. I've traveled to many corners of the world and lived in a number of places. Despite our different languages, habits, styles of expression, values, and choices, if we take the time and pay attention to connect with what's beneath the surface, we find it's our humanity that unites us.

I want to conclude by wishing you all the best on your new assignment. Indulge with curiosity and openness in the richness of the diversity of people and the way they choose to show up on your journey. Learn and enjoy the differences, knowing quite well that deep down, we are all the same.

WORKS REFERENCED

Carucci, Ron. "Leading Change in a Company That's Historically Bad at It." Harvard Business Review, August 6, 2019. https://hbr.org/2019/08/leading-change-in-a-company-thats-historically-bad-at-it.

Cass, Warren. *Influence: How to Raise Your Profile, Manage Your Reputation and Get Noticed.* West Sussex, UK: Wiley, 2017.

Chandler, Steve. *Crazy Good: A Book of CHOICES.* Anna Maria, FL: Maurice Bassett, 2015.

Cross, Rob, and Curt Nickisch. "In a New Role? Here's How to Hit the Ground Running." Produced by Mary Dooe. *HBR IdeaCast,* November 16, 2021. Podcast, MP3 audio, 28:51. https://hbr.org/podcast/2021/11/in-a-new-role-heres-how-to-hit-the-ground-running.

Curcio, Andrew, and Alastair Woods. "Rethinking Total Reward Strategies." *Strategy + Business,* July 27, 2021. https://www.strategy-business.com/article/Rethinking-total-reward-strategies?.

Curcio, Andrew. "The Great Resignation Has Broken Salary Reviews: So How Do Organisations Fix It?" LinkedIn, March 24, 2022. https://www.linkedin.com/pulse/great-resignation-has-broken-salary-reviews-so-how-do-andrew-curcio/.

De Smet, Aaron, Bonnie Dowling, Bryan Hancock, and Bill Schaninger. "The Great Attrition Is Making Hiring Harder. Are You Searching the Right Talent Pools?" *McKinsey Quarterly*, July 13, 2022. https://www.mckinsey.com/capabilities/people-and-organizational-performance/our-insights/the-great-attrition-is-making-hiring-harder-are-you-searching-the-right-talent-pools.

Detert, James R., and Ethan Burris. "Can Your Employees Really Speak Freely?" *Harvard Business Review*, January–February 2016. https://hbr.org/2016/01/can-your-employees-really-speak-freely.

Ewenstein, Boris, Wesley Smith, and Ashvin Sologar. "Changing Change Management." McKinsey & Company. July 1, 2015. https://www.mckinsey.com/featured-insights/leadership/changing-change-management.

Federman, Sarah, and Curt Nickisch. "How Companies Reckon with Past Wrongdoing." Produced by Mary Dooe. *HBR IdeaCast*, January 18, 2022. Podcast, MP3 audio, 25:49. https://hbr.org/podcast/2022/01/how-companies-reckon-with-past-wrongdoing.

Fernández-Aráoz, Claudio, Boris Groysberg, and Nitin Nohria. "How to Hang on to Your High Potentials." *Harvard Business Review*, October 2011. https://hbr.org/2011/10/how-to-hang-on-to-your-high-potentials.

Flaum, J. P. *When It Comes to Business Leadership, Nice Guys Finish First*. Green Peak Partners, 2019. https://greenpeakpartners.com/

wp-content/uploads/2018/09/Green-Peak_Cornell-University-Study_What-predicts-success.pdf.

Gallo, Amy. "The Right Way to Fight." *Harvard Business Review*, May 12, 2010. https://hbr.org/2010/05/the-right-way-to-fight.

Gallup. "Employee Engagement." Accessed February 15, 2023. https://www.gallup.com/394373/indicator-employee-engagement.aspx.

Gino, Francisco. "The Business Case for Curiosity." *Harvard Business Review*, September–October 2018. https://hbr.org/2018/09/the-business-case-for-curiosity.

Goldstone, Lawrence, and Ben Hamer. *The Future of Work, What Workers Want: Winning the War for Talent*. PwC Australia, 2021. https://www.pwc.com.au/important-problems/future-of-work/what-workers-want-report.pdf.

Hurley, Thomas J. *Collaborative Leadership: Engaging Collective Intelligence to Achieve Results across Organisational Boundaries*. White paper. Oxford Leadership, October 2011. https://www.oxfordleadership.com/collaborative-leadership/.

Ibarra, Herminia, and Morten T. Hansen. "Are You a Collaborative Leader?" *Harvard Business Review*, July–August 2011. https://hbr.org/2011/07/are-you-a-collaborative-leader.

Javidan, Mansour, and Aks Zaheer. "How Leaders around the World Build Trust across Cultures." *Harvard Business Review*, May 27, 2019. https://hbr.org/2019/05/how-leaders-around-the-world-build-trust-across-cultures.

Kets de Vries, Manfred F. R. "Are You Ready to Lead Overseas?" INSEAD Knowledge. November 10, 2014. https://knowledge.insead.edu/leadership-organisations/are-you-ready-lead-overseas.

Learnlight. "Why 40% of Overseas Assignments Fail and What You Can Do to Prevent It." May 21, 2018. https://www.learnlight.com/en/articles/overseas-assignments/.

Meyer, Erin, and Sarah Green Carmichael. "How Authority and Decision-Making Differ across Cultures." *HBR IdeaCast*, July 6, 2017. Podcast, MP3 audio, 28:47. https://hbr.org/podcast/2017/07/how-authority-and-decision-making-differ-across-cultures.

Microsoft. *Work Trend Index Annual Report: Great Expectations: Making Hybrid Work Work.* March 16, 2022. https://www.microsoft.com/en-us/worklab/work-trend-index/great-expectations-making-hybrid-work-work.

Neeley, Tsedal, and Sarah Green Carmichael. "Building Successful Hybrid Teams (Back to Work, Better)." Produced by Mary Dooe. *HBR IdeaCast*, July 27, 2021. Podcast, MP3 audio, 28:05. https://hbr.org/podcast/2021/07/building-successful-hybrid-teams.

Neeley, Tsedal, and Sarah Green Carmichael. "Communicate Better with Your Global Team." *HBR IdeaCast*, December 11, 2014. Podcast, MP3 audio, 19:46. https://hbr.org/podcast/2014/12/communicate-better-with-your-global-team.

Rahaman, Saeed, Zia Paton, and Shermarke Howard. *National Compensation Survey 2022: Executive Summary.* PwC Guyana, March 2022. https://www.pwc.com/gy/en/issues/assets/executive-summary-national-compensation-survey-guyana.pdf.

"Self-Awareness: A Key to Better Leadership." *MIT Sloan Management Review*, May 7, 2012. https://sloanreview.mit.edu/article/self-awareness-a-key-to-better-leadership/.

Wilkins, Muriel, and Curt Nickisch. "Taking on a Senior Leadership Role Remotely." Produced by Mary Dooe. *HBR IdeaCast*, February 9, 2021. Podcast, MP3 audio, 29:28. https://hbr.org/podcast/2021/02/taking-on-a-senior-leadership-role-remotely.

ACKNOWLEDGMENTS

MOST OF MY WORK WITH LEADERS AS AN EXECUTIVE COACH happens behind closed doors. I want to express my gratitude to the hundreds of clients who have shared their inner worlds with me over the years. This book is a tribute to their honesty.

I also want to thank my leaders, mentors, and coaches for their guidance, knowledge, and wisdom, and for showing me how true leaders lead. I want to thank the people who openly shared their journeys and stories with me and allowed me to interview them for the book: Ebi Atawodi, Arjan de Boer, Servaas Chorus, Denise Convent, Joost Derickx, Ruth Genota, Assad Gondal, Linda Leu, Umesh Madhyan, Martin Maasland, Bret Packard, and Johan Rolf, as well as those who wish to remain anonymous. A special thanks to Michael Drew, Linda Scott, and Elberti Uiterwaal for powerfully walking their talk. It's inspiring.

A great number of outstanding professionals helped bring this book to life. I want to thank my co-author Peggy Holsclaw, who worked tirelessly despite the many early hours, Darnah Mercieca and her publishing team, who helped me meet publication dead-lines, and Peter Westendorp for his boundless creativity.

Last but not least, I want to express my loving gratitude to Michiel for everything you do for me, always, and to Robin and Simon, who continue to teach me the most valuable leadership lessons every single day.

www.ingramcontent.com/pod-product-compliance
Lightning Source LLC
Chambersburg PA
CBHW022113210326
41597CB00047B/293